Nehemiah Papers

Building a Better America and a Better World

Volume One: 2008 - 2018
With Discussions of "Capitalism-21"

I. M. Nehemiah

I.M. Nehemiah is an allonym for a team of authors (all American citizens) with compilation assistance by Contact Editor Paul S. Anderson, PhD (a retired university professor) who can be contacted at editor@capitalism21.org.

ISBN: 978-1-4834-9047-2 (sc)
ISBN: 978-1-4834-9046-5 (e)

Library of Congress Control Number: 2018910144

The Nehemiah Papers are publicly available at
www.capitalism21.org

Because of the dynamic nature of the Internet, any web addresses or links contained in this book may have changed since publication and may no longer be valid. The views expressed in this work are solely those of the author and do not necessarily reflect the views of the publisher, and the publisher hereby disclaims any responsibility for them.

Any people depicted in stock imagery provided by Getty Images are models, and such images are being used for illustrative purposes only. Certain stock imagery © Getty Images.

Icons used in balance beam images are from Flaticon.com.

Lulu Publishing Services rev. date: 09/27/2018

Dedication

To our future generations who will live in
the world that we are shaping today.

Contents

Suggestions for reading these Nehemiah Papers:

1. Read the Preface first. It helps set the stage.
2. Paper No. 1 is an important introduction. Then choose from the others after reading the suggestions here.
3. Paper No. 14 has four much shorter, more recently written, and more easily readable essays that highlight four major issues. Their strengths rely on the background provided by the other papers.
4. For the lighter side and some political sarcasm, you might consider the two parables in Paper No. 2 in which the messages are still quite serious.
5. Read Paper No. 3 to introduce the Five Realms of Power before you read any of the individual five papers (4 through 8) for greater detail about each Realm of Power.
6. Papers Nos. 11 through 13 are topical about each clearly stated title. Choose what interests you.
7. Papers Nos. 9 and 10 are perhaps the two driest but also the two most important papers. They are not a good place to start reading, but you probably should not leave them to the very end.

Preface -- August 2018

Written in 2008, *Nehemiah Paper* No. 1 starts with these words that are unfortunately as true today in 2018 as they were ten years earlier:

"America is challenged. The calls for "change" are loud from all sides. But changes currently proposed by mainstream leaders (and would-be leaders) seem insufficient, perhaps pathetic in light of the multiple crises facing America in the fall season of 2008."

This current 2018 publication presents the original ten Papers of I. M. Nehemiah that were written in 2008, with three more written in 2010, and with four shorter Articles written in the spring of 2016 that are combined here to become Paper No. 14. These writings are ***intentionally not altered***. They reflect the writings as they were used and summarized in *An Earth Day Carol* (2011), the only other pre-2018 document written by I. M. Nehemiah. That 2011 Carol is not published in this volume because it has been substantially expanded in 2018 to become *A Capitalist Carol*. In the format of historical fiction, *A Capitalist Carol* expresses more completely some of the concepts presented in the original writings of I. M. Nehemiah. *A Capitalist Carol* and the *Nehemiah Papers* are companion volumes that are mutually supportive but are not in a sequence.

A few corrections in punctuation and grammar have been made. Any other notes, alterations or additions to the original fourteen *Nehemiah Papers* are placed in square brackets, such as [... text ...] . However, the original writings did include the occasional use of square brackets [...] in places that have been left unchanged. If in doubt and if the date of any bracketed note is important, consult the original documents that are still maintained and available at www.capitalism21.org, the official website for the *Nehemiah Papers* and for further communications regarding Capitalism-21.

Will there be more writings by I. M. Nehemiah?

There are no restrictions. Any or all or none of the following are possible:

A. Preliminary drafts of Papers 15 through 20 exist. If any of them are released (and not necessarily in the same numbered order), they would be updated for the currents times, that is, 2018 or later.

B. Updated versions of the fourteen Papers could be written and released, but only with clear indication that they are contemporary writings, such as being named "Nehemiah Paper No. 5 – Revised 2018". Several of the Papers need to be updated to include concepts and explanations that are currently only expressed in the fictional story *A Capitalist Carol*.

C. Because I. M. Nehemiah is an allonym for undisclosed authors, additional contributors could be included, and original ones might withdraw from the group. Any action about what is released under the name of I. M. Nehemiah is a collaborative decision, with current communications via the Contact Editor.

D. Future writings will depend in part on the impact or lack of impact of this current release of the original writings. Maybe America does not care about such issues. If so, then so be it. But if Americans or citizens of any nation become interested to discuss the concepts of Capitalism-21 and to take steps toward implementation, additional writings by I. M. Nehemiah are likely.

The Nehemiah of ancient times was a builder, not a fiery prophet of gloom and doom. Modern I. M. Nehemiah also seeks to build. The problems and solutions that I. M. Nehemiah presents are in the hands of Americans, at least until other countries or Mother Nature get into the act.

Best wishes to America and to all other countries and people. This is more than just about America. It is about everyone and the entire planet.

I.M.N.

Introduction to the Nehemiah Papers
[Paper No. 1 of the Nehemiah Papers]
I. M. Nehemiah © October 2008

Preamble:

America is challenged. The calls for "change" are loud from all sides. But changes currently proposed by mainstream leaders (and would-be leaders) seem insufficient, perhaps pathetic in light of the multiple crises facing America in the fall season of 2008. The *Nehemiah Papers* are an attempt to clarify the true challenges and propose solutions. Very little time remains to discuss and debate in advance of voter action. Regardless who wins, the election alone cannot resolve the issues and challenges America faces today. Tangible solutions beyond political rhetoric are required in the most immediate sense. The proposed solutions in the *Nehemiah Papers* challenge Americans in significant ways and require change in the course our nation is following. How all candidates and especially the victors in this and future elections respond to the issues raised here will tell us much about them, possibly alter our voting patterns, and certainly impact our future (for better or worse). And every future time votes are cast and counted, we will know much more about ourselves and whether we collectively as a nation have the courage to shape our own destiny. *I.M.N.*

Introduction:

Whether by the grace of God or the wonders of evolution, the highest marks of Humankind are the abilities to reason and to utilize those thoughts intentionally to modify the environment, society, and even oneself. Unfortunately, the lowest marks of Humankind are the human tendencies for selfishness and reluctance to make self-improving corrections.

In 1991, after several years of internal turmoil and external pressures, the non-democratic Soviet Union voluntarily broke apart and ended the greatest (but also flawed) experiment of socialism. This voluntary shift came largely as a surprise, altered the course of history, and marked a high-point in both peaceful reasoning and intentional modification of governance and economics at the level of great nations. Democracy and capitalism have been declared the victors, and rightly so. But whether democracy and capitalism can also self-evaluate and adjust remains to be seen.

America is now the self-appointed "high priest" of both democratic governance and capitalist economics. With its super-power status and influence, America leads many people, societies, and nations, both rich and poor, with the American models of democracy and capitalism. What is written in these Papers about America can be interpreted and adjusted for many nations of the World, including parliamentary democracies (some with a limited monarchy) and even "pseudo-democracies" with vastly lopsided power structures and old-fashion abusive capitalism.

Now, in 2008, the American versions of democracy and capitalism are challenged not only in this book (written in early 2008 and revised in October), but also in the real world. Democracy and capitalism are not to be abandoned, but rather the reasoned *Nehemiah Papers* propose some very distinctive modifications. What remains to be seen is if America can accomplish its needed self-corrections, or will it ride its present course in a downward spiral. That spiral includes the negative elements of self-centered greed, an unjustified beaconing of prideful superiority, enormous personal and national debts, and a lack of self-discipline by individuals, corporations, elected officials, and the nation as a whole. Each of these negative elements can be brought under control by improved American democracy and

"Capitalism-21," a variation of capitalism appropriate for the 21st Century and proposed in these Papers.

The Briefest Summary:

The following eight statements comprise a very condensed summation that unfortunately runs the danger of being overly simplified. Subsequent Papers provide requisite support and expanded explanations of these initial statements.

1. **The American dilemma:** America is facing an impending (already started?) decline with massive consequences. The nation is seriously challenged from outside and within, and what needs to be done requires some introspection and then actions different from the standard alternatives currently offered by the two major American political parties.

2. **The proposed actions borrow the best from both political parties** and reject the worst from each. Building a stronger and better America is not as simple as liberal Democrats (the moderate to far left) and conservative Republicans (the moderate to far right) would have us believe.

3. **Concerning economic issues, American capitalism presents a dilemma with two sides:**
   - More government influence and social control on wealth (as in higher taxes and more government-directed programs, as proposed generally by the left), versus
   - Less government control of capitalistic business (as in lower taxes and less government-sponsored assistance or protections, as proposed generally by the right).

4. **Concerning issues of governance, American lifestyles (including religious, moral and legal-protection issues) present another dilemma with two sides:**
   - More "lifestyle latitude" and freedoms (as proposed generally by the left), versus

- More morality and social constraints (as proposed generally by the right).

5. **The Nehemiah writings advocate a combination** that is primarily liberal left on the economic (capitalism) aspects and primarily conservative right on the life-style (democracy) aspects. That might seem like a strange combination, but there are rational explanations in the Papers.

6. **The Nehemiah proposals reject the extremists** at both ends of each set of issues.

    A. On capitalism: There is no intention to destroy or even modify the core components of capitalism in America as experienced by the middle 80% of Americans.

    Assistance programs for the poor are not to be free handouts without requiring responsibility in appropriate ways. But at the other end, the powers of the wealthy are challenged, and controls are sought via voluntary actions backed up by tax laws. The wealthy should bear increased social responsibility as a consequence of their good fortune.

    B. On democracy: There is no intention of allowing religious zealots to impose their morality on everyone. Likewise, the extreme attacks on America's core life-styles and values by secular liberal efforts in courtrooms, profit-obsessed media, and vice-peddling criminals are rejected as being detrimental to the well-being of Americans and our country. A democratically-determined preservation and strengthening of the core ethical values upon which America was founded is of immense importance.

7. In the final analysis, **the Nehemiah Papers are about controlling a range of excesses both in capitalist economics and in democratically definable social behavior.** The two go together because the extra revenues (tax reform with targeted deductions) from the excesses of capitalism can be used to resolve (perhaps with "charter neighborhoods") the critical social ills of American poverty. The ultimate benefit would be a stronger American economy with new and sustainable employment, usefully directed cash flows, and less waste. Volunteerism is to be raised to new heights

in America, including compulsory national service for all men and women who do not volunteer. Strict term limits on elected officials will help bring America's governance back on track, that is, back into the hands of the people. And international policies that are more equitable (not so USA-centered) will promote worldwide cooperation and peace.

⟡⟡⟡⟡⟡⟡⟡⟡⟡⟡⟡⟡⟡⟡⟡⟡⟡⟡⟡⟡⟡⟡⟡⟡⟡⟡⟡⟡⟡⟡⟡⟡⟡⟡⟡⟡⟡⟡

The Nehemiah Papers are about controlling a range of excesses both in capitalist economics and in democratically definable social behavior.

⟡⟡⟡⟡⟡⟡⟡⟡⟡⟡⟡⟡⟡⟡⟡⟡⟡⟡⟡⟡⟡⟡⟡⟡⟡⟡⟡⟡⟡⟡⟡⟡⟡⟡⟡⟡⟡⟡

8. **The international implications** of these approaches should be notably beneficial to every person and nation that collaborates with the efforts for 21st Century reforms of democracy and capitalism.

The Goals of the I. M. Nehemiah

Goal 1. Define a minimally acceptable standard of living and elevate all people who are below that level in America and in the World, while ensuring no dire hardships are imposed on other citizens. Paper No. 13 examines the full range of existing living conditions and sets the minimum level quite low, yet high enough to give people a reasonable chance for fairness. However, that level will not be attained easily in many areas.

Goal 2. Find the human and monetary resources to accomplish Goal 1. The proposed solutions are **through the implementation of Capitalism-21,** a more equitable ("fair") and responsive variation than is our current Capitalism-20. See Papers No. 5, No. 11, and No. 20. The very wealthy contribute most of the funding, with some options for them to direct the expenditures. They will not suffer; rather, they may gain as the economy grows. The wealthy can be champions or by-standers, but they cannot veto actions decided by democratic processes.

Goal 3. Facilitate the implementation of Capitalism-21 and the minimum acceptable living conditions **by re-balancing the Five Realms of Power** that impact and control America. This includes restricting the influence of money and "serial incumbents" while strengthening ethics and core values, providing for enforcement of fair laws, and elevating personal service to the level of a respected "currency" as a partial balance to the power of money. Many of the Papers relate to this goal.

Goal 4. Improve the future lives of all Americans by eliminating the worst of our society, facilitating similar improvements in nations that decide to cooperate, and thereby **avoiding the otherwise inevitable serious decline of America** as a leading and prosperous nation. All parts of the *Nehemiah Papers* deal with this goal.

Join the above **boldface** words to produce one **Super-Goal:**

Define a minimally acceptable standard of living and elevate all people who are below that level through the implementation of Capitalism-21 by re-balancing the Five Realms of Power [to] improve the future lives of all Americans [by] avoiding the otherwise inevitable serious decline of America.

Ambitious? Yes! But the alternatives are dreadful.

> *"Make no small plans, for they have no power to stir the soul."*
> [Niccolo Machiavelli]

Historical Background:

In 1787-88, eighty-five essays were published as the *Federalist Papers* advocating the ratification of the Constitution of the United States of America. Although written by Alexander Hamilton, James Madison and John Jay, the essays were printed under the allonym (a pseudonym based on an historical person) of *"Publius"* in honor of a Roman consul influential in establishing the Roman Republic around 500 B.C.

The allonym *"Nehemiah"* is in honor of the Hebrew leader instrumental in the rebuilding of Jerusalem around 440 B.C. Ancient Nehemiah was a builder of a nation; modern Nehemiah is trying to be a builder of America and the World community. The initials I. M. have been added to give a more modern and personal touch. The writings of I. M. Nehemiah are by one or more highly patriotic adult American citizens who choose to remain anonymous.

◇◇

I. M. Nehemiah is one or more highly patriotic adult American citizens who choose to remain anonymous.

◇◇

Interestingly, the *Federalist No. 10* essay warns of how factions (or parties) in a nation can obtain power and distort the workings of democracy. I. M. Nehemiah states the case that a faction that opposes controls upon capitalism in America has obtained unusual and considerably unfair power over American democracy. The faction uses its money and assets for intentional influence upon our elected "serial incumbent" government, resulting in laws with a bias favorable to massive wealth and unfavorable to basic fairness for sub-lower-class citizens. The "middle class" citizens are lulled by commercialism and materialism into accepting this doubly-unjust arrangement.

Similar to the *Federalist Papers*, the essays of I. M. Nehemiah are not legalistic or academic arguments. Rather, the *Nehemiah Papers* are statements to the American people, the common citizens, the voters. The future well-being of America is of great personal interest to us all. And adjustments need to be made very soon. In fact, they are long overdue. I hope we are not too late.

Listing of the Papers:

The *Nehemiah Papers* (of October 2008) is [intended to be] a series of twenty essays about *Building a Better America and a Better World.* In brief, there are four Blocks of essays. Block A presents the basic information quickly and succinctly. Block B provides more detailed information and arguments about the Five Realms of Power and the Nehemiah proposals. Block C contains separate, freestanding essays about important issues in America today, including their genesis, history, and projections about our future. Block D provides plans for action.

Block A. The Basics

Paper No. 1: *Introduction to the* Nehemiah Papers

Includes this table of contents.

Paper No .2: *The Parable of a Great Nation*

[Two stories] with political satire and lessons.

Paper No. 3: *The Five Realms of Power: An Introduction*

A possible key for real change.

Block B. More about the Five Realms of Power, plus the Postulates and Proposals

Paper No. 4: *Governance and Democracy*

Votes that should rule but do not.

Paper No. 5: *Economics and Capitalism*

The power of money and Capitalism-21.

Paper No. 6: *Religion and Faith*

Not a tidy package.

Paper No .7: *Justice and Law*

Laws are made to be changed.

Paper No. 8: *Love and Caring*

A possible counter-force to money.

Paper No. 9: *The Nehemiah Postulates*

Fifteen statements upon which these Papers are based.

Summarized to only five, they are:

- A. America is heading for a life-changing decline.
- B. The Five Realms of Power are out of balance in America.
- C. American capitalism incorrectly dominates American democracy.
- D. The impending decline can be averted through democratic revisions of our laws.
- E. Service should be invoked as a "currency" to balance the power of money.

Paper No. 10: *The Nehemiah Proposals*

Ten proposals to tackle the challenges to America.

Block C. Supporting Essays about the Proposals and Other Important Issues

Paper No.11: Equality and Justice in a Capitalist Democracy
 The equality problem.
Paper No.12: Sources of Wealth in America
 How wealth has been accumulated.
Paper No.13: Poverty in America and the World
 It is all relative, but it is severe.
Paper No.14: Four [Articles]
 [Shorter writings to introduce issues in 2016.]
[Note: The Articles replace what was to be Paper 14: *Four Stories* Plausible fiction to help understand the options.]

Block D. Possibilities for Action, plus the Conclusion

[**NOTE: Papers 15 through 20 were not finalized and not released.**]

Paper No.15: Problem Neighborhoods
 "Charter neighborhoods" for our communities.
Paper No.16: In a World at Peace
 Development of "charter nations."
Paper No.17: In a World at War – Part 1: Iraq
 A plan for democracy.
Paper No.18: In a World at War – Part 2: Israel and Palestine
 A plan for peace.
Paper No.19: Concluding Remarks as of October 2008
 Summary.
Paper No.20: Capitalism-21 and Political Remarks as of October 2008
 Comments on candidates and influential people.
Appendix: Who is I. M. Nehemiah?
 One or more patriotic adult American citizens.

* * * * * * *

Note: Although presented in the context of America, the content of the *Nehemiah Papers* is similarly relevant to all affluent nations and all pockets of affluent people in other nations around the World.

I hope you enjoy the writings. I hope they will stir you to action. I feel compelled to present these writings because

I. M. Nehemiah
Builder of a better America and a better World

The Parable[s] of a Great Nation
[Paper No. 2-A of the Nehemiah Papers]
I. M. Nehemiah © October 2008

[There was only one parable written before the US presidential election of 2008. The second parable was written before the mid-term congressional elections of 2010.]

Parable 2008: The Shrub Years

Note: This is an old story retold in the context of America in 2008. Other versions of this story are also possible about previous administrations. America has needed this message for many decades. IMN

There once was a prosperous Great Nation. The people selected the men and women who ruled it. Some rulers were very good; some were not. By tradition, the candidates to be ruler made major efforts to distinguish themselves from each other, but all were surprisingly similar, partly to appeal to the central majority of the people.

The current ruler named Shrub had been blessed by being the son of a previous ruler who had the blessing of being the ideological son of an even earlier ruler who was almost regal. This was as close to a dynasty as had been seen in this nation. Ruler Shrub was highly opinionated and inclined toward personal feelings of right and wrong.

But who would carry on the dynasty? Because he had no sons to indoctrinate with his thinking, he looked at his twin daughters and said: "The two

11

men who can each tell me an absolute truth shall join my family, and I shall prepare them to be rulers someday."

Many men came forth with their truths to be evaluated by the ruler. Of course, each one was thoroughly screened by the ruler's security forces.

Bachelor #1 was handsome, a past-president of his college fraternity, and a good talker. Ruler Shrub and his daughters liked him. He said: "The waters of the oceans shall flow forever." The ruler consulted experts who pointed out that water freezes and that the Arctic Ocean is virtually covered with solid ice. Ruler Shrub called on a scientific commission to verify this, and only then he accepted the findings (although he was habitually doubtful of scientific commissions). So Bachelor #1 was rejected by Ruler Shrub in spite of his protests that water under the Arctic ice stays liquid and does move a little. The ruler said: "No. Close, but no cigar," a jestful reference to old contests to win a cigar. The twins were not happy.

Bachelor #2 was similarly handsome and social, but more rugged, an outdoors type. The twins liked him also. He said: "The natural environment that sustains us is fragile and deserves major efforts for protection." A cheer went up from the environmentalists led by a prior candidate for ruler who had been gored in a previous selection. But key advisors to Ruler Shrub quickly pointed out how the prosperity of the nation depended greatly on current rates of use of natural resources and that the "green-minded" protectionists were fanatics (and some truly were) who were overlooking the ability of science and technology to solve the problems. Ruler Shrub weighed the evidence (but only for a minute or two because he had already decided about such matters many years before) and said: "No. Close, but just a cigar," a less-than-jestful reference to a previous ruler who had made some poor personal decisions.

The third man was Mr. Burton, a plump, bald, older fellow. Because of his age and prior marital status, the term "bachelor" was dropped. Candidate #3 said: "The powers of our businesses, sciences, finances, military and energy sectors assure us of continued and expanding greatness provided we take forceful measures for their continued strengths." That was the short version. Actually, Mr. Burton spoke on and on, citing examples of how the current and previous rulers of the dynasty had taken such measures to maintain greatness, noting the break-up of the nation's major rival by out-spending it [and driving up the national debt, which he did not mention]. He also cited expert testimony provided by business and energy management. There was no need to listen to any other "experts." Of course Ruler Shrub and his advisors were highly impressed. But the twins were terrified. They begged their father to reject him. The ruler said: "Well, I must accept his absolute truth; it is exactly what I know to be true. But I will make him my vice-ruler and the intermediate heir-apparent while we continue the search." The twins breathed a sigh of relief. And that is how Mr. Hal E. Burton became vice-ruler, only a heartbeat away from ruling the Great Nation.

Several dozen more candidates presented their absolute truths that related to love, patriotism, interest rates, ethnicity, science and much more. All were rejected, even the ones about the inevitability of death and taxes, about which Ruler Shrub cited the possible "Rapture" and declared he would someday eliminate taxes because businesses and wealthy people would surely agree to voluntarily sustain the nation.

One candidate had an absolute truth that "there is no perfect security system." This was proven to be correct by revealing he was actually a cross-dresser (a female transvestite). The revelation touched off a flurry of controversy on historically taboo issues ranging from gender identity to same-sex marriage. Facing investigation, each of the security agencies promptly claimed it knew about him (her) all the time but was testing the other agencies. Ruler Shrub accepted the agencies' claims, and therefore, this candidate's "truth" was not absolute.

<><><><><><><><><><><><><><><><><><><><><><><><><><><><><><><><><>

Eventually everyone lost count of the number of candidates, so the next fellow became the "nth" candidate, or Candidate "N."

<><><><><><><><><><><><><><><><><><><><><><><><><><><><><><><><><>

Eventually everyone lost count of the number of candidates, so the next fellow became the "nth" candidate, or Candidate "N." Candidate "N" presented himself in a manner quite unlike the prior ones; he just seemed to appear, make his statement, and depart. Afterwards, some thought he was old; others thought he was young. He could have been a divorcee, widower, single, or even married. He could have been a member of any church, either rich or poor, and even of undetermined ethnic/racial origin.

Perhaps he was a she, but nobody wanted to raise that question. And he might even have been two or more people that were acting as a single author of his statement. Candidate "N" was an enigma, without a name. So he became known as "N," the "N-igma." Two details about himself that he clearly stated were that he dearly loved the Great Nation and was absolutely patriotic.

To the ruler and the people of the nation, Candidate "N" stated his absolute truth: "Throughout the history of this World, all previous powerful and prosperous nations have weakened and fallen, and -(making a slow sweeping gesture with his arm to indicate the grandeur of the Great Nation)- all this, too, shall pass away."

After a moment of stunned silence, everyone erupted in discussion and outcries. The prosperous future of the nation had been questioned. The continuation of the world-leading power of the Great Nation had been challenged. The abilities of the ruler and all future rulers had been doubted. The vision of the long-term welfare of the people had been shaken.

The security forces could not produce any files on Candidate "N," but questioned his patriotism. A news station showed its video from a side angle to make it appear that the sweeping gesture was intended as a physical slap to the ruler. Ruler Shrub declared an end to the search for absolute truths, and the twins were happy to reconsider Candidates #1 and #2.

And Candidate "N"? He said to a few people close to him that he would return when the Great Nation was more receptive of ways to meet the inevitable challenges of the future. Then he just disappeared as quickly as he had arrived. He blended into the population of the nation quite naturally, being so non-distinct in age, appearance, background, and possibly number (surely "N" did not act alone). But whoever he or she or they were was not important. The message had been delivered.

To his (or her or their) credit, Candidate "N" remained unknown and never tried to gain fame or high office or fortune from that initial appearance. Some say she died soon after. Others swore he was an escapee from a prison for mentally insane criminals and was soon recaptured. Others stepped forward claiming to be Candidate "N," but none could convince the people.

In truth, Candidate "N" could have been "N-ee-one," "N-ee-body," or "N-ee messenger." To some people, he/she/they were the "N-emy." Some spoke poorly of this "N-tee-Christ" because they believed themselves to be God's chosen people. The ruler and many other leaders vowed that such a decline in the Great Nation would never occur under his reign or future reigns of "true patriots" who thought and acted as they did.

Some agreed with "N," but felt powerless. Some even proclaimed the impending decline, but sounded like ancient Hebrew prophets of doom, such as Noah, Lot, Jeremiah, and Jonah.

The Great Nation was still strong and prosperous, and responses to the challenge of Candidate "N" were numerous and quite predictable. The military requested more of the national budget; big business guaranteed that less government control would assure prosperity; and the wealthy lobbied that lower taxes for them would benefit the nation. Religious leaders called for repentance while assuring believers that God would preserve the Great Nation; labor unions called for higher wages for their workers as a sure economic stimulus; and everyone sponsored patriotic parades. But no changes of lasting impact were made, and the Great Nation continued on its multi-decade course of perceived, unlimited greatness while heading almost blindly toward eventual decline.

Diverse groups with their left and right perspectives kept calling for "change." Two leaders known as "M" and "O" (as close as either could get to "N") rose to prominence, but they were viewed suspiciously, even as new indicators of socio-economic difficulties became fearsomely evident. Unfortunately, as increased trials and tribulations did fall upon the Great Nation, many people thought that neither seemed to address the crisis with sufficient urgency, except as needed to garner enough votes to be selected as the next ruler.

* * * * * * * *

And what about "N"? He said that he would someday speak again and try to help the Great Nation in a time of need. Certainly any nation is in serious trouble when it is engaged in two wars, has over thirty percent decline in its stock market, has over ten trillion dollars of national debt, has massive yearly deficit spending, has financial crises in home mortgages, and has looming disasters with credit card debt and near insolvency of some state governments and pension plans. Compounding such troubles are an energy crisis, fifteen percent of the nation's most vulnerable citizens without health coverage, and plagues of greed, conspicuous consumption, low morality, declining education, unbalanced social well-being, and more. Perhaps worst of all are sequential incumbents who seek reelection more than they seek viable and forceful changes that any nation must undergo if it is to reverse the clear trends of decline.

◇◇◇

Is the Great Nation ready for any more messages from "N"?

◇◇◇

Is the Great Nation ready for any more messages from "N"? The response to the Papers released in October 2008 will tell "N" if her other writings are now appropriate for publication.

First, a few questions and comments for "M" and "O": [M for McCain and O for Obama.]

1. **Health care:**
   A. Dear "M": If a financially-challenged person does not owe any income tax, how does a $5000 tax credit help him or her obtain health care coverage? Some see this as pandering to those in the middle-class who might let impoverished fellow citizens remain without health care.
   B. Dear "O": Why would universal health care coverage be proposed at a high level equal to that of well-paid elected officials when funding for such is clearly not available? Be realistic. People with money and/or strong employment should be able to choose to pay for better services, but those with little or no money should have enough assistance for simple and decent coverage (such as basic clinics) without resorting to emergency rooms or charitable health care assistance. Suggestion: Build up from the basics instead of promising the moon.

2. **Education:**
   A. Dear "M": In the District of Columbia there are about 59,000 students, and let's consider for discussion that 30,000 are in "less-than-favorable" schools. Vouchers would allow parents/

students to choose more-favored schools. But if there were (as you stated) 9000 applicants for 1000 vouchers, what happens to the other 8000 who would not get vouchers, or the other 21,000 who did not choose to enter this "lottery" for better education? Even providing 5000 vouchers would hardly address the magnitude of changes needed in DC education.

B. Dear "O": Would you agree on the need to reach far beyond your current rhetoric if you expect to improve education in truly problematic schools? The roots of poor schooling are most evident in disadvantaged neighborhoods where many parents are either detached from the goals of education or possibly resistant to some of the widely held core values of the Great Nation.

3. **Taxes and income redistribution:** Dear "M" and "O": Please respond to this:

A. When Mark the Marketer, Sally the Seamstress, or Paul the Plumber have taxable incomes over $250,000, their comfortable lifestyles should be relatively unaffected even if taxed at 50% on any *additional income.* If such a person earns an additional hundred thousand taxable-dollars (even after massive deductions that would encourage job creation and investment in equipment, *etc.*), maybe he or she could be happy keeping only an **extra** $50,000 more each year than what most citizens have. Note: Multiply these numbers by 10 for million-dollar incomes, and by 100 for those mentioned in the next paragraph. When the wealthy are not satisfied with that much after-tax income (plus their prestige and power), it illustrates the very problematic core of wayward capitalism, the greedy capitalism where the wealthy can never have enough.

B. Actually it is Harry the Hedgefunder, Cheryl the Celebrity, and Ernie the Executive who are making the really big money, and they know (or can hire) the accounting methods to lawfully reduce their taxable incomes. Because there are so many ways to legally manipulate and lower the taxes on both persons and corporations, the citizens of the Great Nation are not really paying overly high tax rates. A nation does not function without "cash flow." Taxes are national incomes that become national expenditures for the national well-being. Certainly Government must be held accountable to use money and resources in ways to appropriately benefit all citizens, including the wealthy, but not in ways that favor exaggerated accumulation of more wealth (net worth, not just annual income) while other national needs are neglected.

C. The fear-mongering comments about taxes as "income redistribution" perpetrate a cruel joke on the middle class that votes to lower taxes on the wealthy. Nobody is advocating financial equality for all citizens. Rather, most citizens would embrace some degree of equity (meaning "fairness") as being desirable. Recall that progressive taxes were even advocated by Adam Smith, the first great champion of Capitalism. De-regulation and trickle-down prosperity in capitalist economics can appear favorable during times of economic expansion, but they fail the test of "fairness" when times get tough. The wealthy will always protect themselves first, even while they appear to be generous to the poor. A humane government is essential. (And "humane" is not a socialist word; "humane" relates to the nice side of being human.)

4. **Greed and the "Great Nation Dream":** Again "M" and "O" are invited to comment:

A. Unlimited dreams and unlimited greed can go hand-in-hand. It is wonderful that some people actually do rise spectacularly in the Great Nation, but fame and/or enormous wealth should not be so elevated that they distort the moral fabric of our culture. And such success should not occur at the expense of the public, especially not of the very disadvantaged individuals in unsafe neighborhoods with poor schools and high unemployment. (You know those places; they are where most people, including you, would not want to live.)

B. The real "Great Nation Dream" is for sound education, respectful health care, safety in all neighborhoods, available healthy food, reasonable housing, and honorable employment. Prospects for attaining that dream attract quality immigrants to our nation. Prospects for outlandish success are also attractive, but should never be the essence of our culture.

<u>Second, a selection of other topics important to "N":</u>

5. **Service:**
   A. The Great Nation should require at least twelve months of modestly-paid national service (military, Peace Corps, teaching, social work, neighborhood improvement, law enforcement, and many more options) by every male and female between 18 and 30 years of age. This is great for creating new jobs, providing training/experience in the formative years, and getting important work done. Furthermore, appropriate to their circumstances and prior service, there should be retroactive required service (perhaps unpaid) for all persons between 30 and 55 years of age. The citizens need to awaken to the fact that things must change, and that they (not just their fellow citizens) must do something and must actually sacrifice something.

6. **Term limits:**
   A. The "professional" politicians have failed us time and time again. "N" calls them "serial incumbents" and proposes limits on sequential re-election. After one term, the politician can seek a different office (perhaps in state or local government) or actually have merit-based (not voter-based) employment in business or government. Then, at least one election later, he or she would be eligible to run for the position held initially.

7. **Many more topics** will be discussed if requested, including:
   A. "The Five Realms of Power" and their Five "Currencies";
   B. "Charter Neighborhoods";
   C. Sources of Wealth;
   D. Poverty in the Great Nation and Abroad;
   E. Foreign Policies; and
   F. A proposal for "Capitalism-21" appropriate for our new century.

In conclusion, best wishes to the Great Nation. Avoiding decline will not be easy, but it will be worth the effort.

I. M. N.

The Parable[s] of a Great Nation
[Paper No. 2-B of the Nehemiah Papers]
I. M. Nehemiah © August 2010

Parable 2010: The Weecan Years

There once was a prosperous Great Nation. Its people were led for many years by Ruler Shrub and his political allies, the Pachyderms. They had many followers during a period of great affluence. Revenues were strong (as had been shown by the previous ruler) but spectacularly insufficient when the Great Nation fought two wars while lowering income tax rates, especially on the wealthy. Money flowed freely, some great fortunes were made, the stock market raced higher and higher, and loans on houses were wonderfully easy to obtain. It was a good time to be in debt. How could anything go wrong?

But difficulties came quickly, like the bursting of a bubble. Although still a Great Nation, its troubles included the two wars, over thirty percent decline in its stock market, over ten trillion dollars of national debt, massive yearly deficit spending, unfavorable balance of trade, financial crises in home mortgages, looming disasters with credit card debt, and near insolvency of some state governments and pension plans. Compounding such troubles were an energy crisis, fifteen percent of the nation's most vulnerable citizens without health coverage, and plagues of greed, conspicuous consumption, lowered morality, declining education, unbalanced social well-being, and more.

As Ruler Shrub's reign came to a close, the Pachyderms chose a big Mac as their leader in the forthcoming elections. They advocated lower taxes, school vouchers, and private health insurance, which to some people seemed like lipstick on a pig wallowing into a great recession.

The other major political group, the Equines, vehemently called for change and even selected a candidate with a very strange name, Mr. Oyes Weecan. Promises, promises. Like universal health care equal to that of the national legislators (absurd). And including in the middle class those with net taxable incomes three to five times what a professional schoolteacher typically earns.

Both candidates were viewed suspiciously, even as new indicators of socio-economic difficulties became fearsomely evident. As increased trials and tribulations did fall upon the Great Nation, many people thought that neither seemed to address the crisis with sufficient urgency, except as needed to garner enough votes to be selected as the next ruler.

The victorious Ruler Weecan inherited all of the problems from Ruler Shrub and from all the previous rulers. To shake off the difficulties of the economic downturn, the Equine majority in the legislature set out to do what they knew best: to spend and to regulate (and eventually to tax the wealthy if they could). Considering the excessive de-regulation of previous decades, some rules were placed on the supposedly self-regulated financial sector that caused so much of the recent problems, but only after magnificent bailouts were provided to some entities "too big to fail." And, as the overall economy withered, funds for "recovery projects" pumped money into the pockets of the fortunate few, such as shovel-ready highway construction firms and nearly-bankrupt state governments that were also poor managers of their funds. The jobs and the funds were to trickle down to the people. What little recovery there was faced constant challenges and threats, some even from greasy economies overseas.

Meanwhile, the Pachyderms simply lined up trunk-to-tail to attempt to block the Equine initiatives. Voting was strictly along party lines, with nearly all legislators representing their ideologies and not their constituencies. (But that is how they got elected, and their first priority seemed to be getting reelected.)

The Pachyderms were well aware that blocking tactics and criticisms of the Weecan efforts could eventually attract sufficient dissatisfaction that the political tides would shift, as they always do in this democracy.

Elections typically have been the choosing of the lesser of two evils. During improving times, the incumbents have an advantage. But during declining or insufficiently improving times, those in power have a disadvantage. So the Pachyderms became the party of "Nope" and reaped benefits for doing nothing except advocating the return to policies that had contributed so much to the problems at hand.

Finally, in a self-serving show of bipartisan unity (because each wanted to claim leadership with the solutions), the Equines and Pachyderms issued a joint call for proposals to resolve the challenges facing the Great Nation. Many of the Equines and Pachyderms spoke up (and were happy to be visible to the public), but all were basically quite similar. Neither side could see much further than the next election. And the political leaders knew that the people of the Great Nation were interested mainly in their own affluence, so the keys to power were tied largely to self-serving, short-term, minimal-effort, minimal-discomfort solutions. The proposals basically were hagglings about rates of taxation, government approaches to international affairs including war and world leadership, and issues of social liberty such as abortions, guns, prayers, and education. In other words, the proposals were much like what had been said before. And the economy continued to struggle, with indicators of further decline. Solutions were absent. The rhetoric was as much negative about the opposition as it was self-patronizing compliments.

The enigmatic "N" decided to come forth again, this time in writings via the Internet. He (or she or they) presented the following:

◇◇◇

"And all this too shall pass away"

◇◇◇

"And all this too shall pass away" was again emphasized. One hundred years of world leadership is but a blink in history, and decline is already beginning to be evident.

There is no possible way to return the economy to the heydays of luxury living, fat portfolios for retirement, and seemingly endless prosperity. That should not be our objective, because it is selfish and would lead to continuing problems that brought on the current difficulties.

The roots of the problems of the Great Nation are found where the "Five

Realms of Power" are out of balance. 1) The Economics of Captitalism-20 plays favorites to those with wealth, giving inappropriate influence over 2) Governance by Democracy. [Government is excessively influenced by money.] The power of 3) Religion is being distorted by extremes of both the conservative and liberal Faiths, while 4) Justice through Laws is being manipulated to favor the wealthy and the politically powerful. [Polarized opinions are warping the legal system to be supportive of favoritism and inequalities inherent in "Capitalism-20."]

◇◇◇

Interestingly, the weakest Realm, the power of Love with Service, offers the greatest hope for bringing the Five Realms of Power back into balance.

◇◇◇

Interestingly, the weakest Realm, the power of 5) Love with Service, offers the greatest hope for bringing the five realms of power back into balance. [Meaningful, non-monetary recognition and reward for service should massively offset the power of money to influence public policy and societal behavior.]

Clearly, those few sentences could not present the full reasoning, so "N" announced the availability of the "Nehemiah Papers" on the Internet, with access via the Facebook page entitled, "Nehemiah Papers."

At first, nothing happened. Too few readers; nobody helped bring the Papers to the attention of the public. And "N" was essentially unheard. Then "N" tried to reach the public through the ageless tradition of parables and parodies. She did not expect stalwart Pachyderms and Equines to assist much, but there were hopes that freethinkers might make the Nehemiah Papers better known. "N" only wanted those writings to be openly discussed by the Great Nation. She sought neither recognition nor personal involvement beyond her written statements.

The Nehemiah Papers contain nothing inflammatory and no personal attacks. Just some soundly reasoned observations that look into the heart of the Great Nation to understand the causes of its problems and the prospects of continuing decline or possible stability. Other topics and proposals by "N" include:

1. A definition and basic proposal for "Capitalism-21" appropriate for our new century, intending to balance better the Five Realms of Power.

2. An equitable system for compulsory national service for everyone (male and female) age 18 to 55, with major impact on job creation, training, and solution of some national problems, with some allowances for service by teachers, police, and other public servants with earnings under a set maximum or in hardship areas.

3. Seventy-five percent (75%) tax bracket for income over a million dollars but allowing some taxpayer influence on the use of the high-bracket funds, such as efforts for Charter Neighborhoods.

4. "Charter Neighborhoods" to improve locations where most people would not want to live, including massive campaigns against crime, drugs, and corruption.

5. Job creation in education, public safety, social work, and fields that strengthen the nation's qualities, not its quantities.

6. Creation of jobs and industry for environmentally sound solutions to the energy issues, again building the nation instead of shipping its wealth overseas.

7. Sources of Wealth, to understand the nature of wealth and its responsibilities.

8. Poverty in the Great Nation and Abroad, to show that even the "middle class" is highly privileged and needs to consider the necessary sacrifices to prevent an otherwise unavoidable decline.

9. Restrictions on the welfare system and revisions of health care, but strengthening the minimal base services to all people.

10. Elimination of "serial incumbents" who seek reelection more than they seek viable and forceful changes, either by term limits or rejection by voters.

11. Creation of "moderate politics" either by the rise of a new political party, the election of independents, or by the empowerment of moderates within their existing parties.

12. Foreign policies consistent with the values of I. M. Nehemiah.

13. Implementation of long-term solutions, many of which would be popular only when true leadership surfaces in the Great Nation,

while rejecting the temptations of short–term power or financial gain.

* * * * * *

"N" emphasized that the current pathways of the Great Nation were leading to decline, and that drastic changes were needed immediately to delay or possibly avoid that decline. But the needed steps would involve sacrifices so significant that no former leading nation had ever implemented them in time to maintain its position of greatness.

Is the Great Nation ready for these and other messages from "N"? The response to the Nehemiah Papers released in August–October 2010 will either have zero impact or could set the flavor for the coming political session when the Great Nation tries to correct its course.

Then, Ruler Weecan, the other elected leaders, and the concerned people will show if they are able to steer the Ship of State from the brink of unrecoverable decline onto a course for continued (but different) greatness. As "N" says: "We must never be the same again."

And what about "N"? He, she or they continue to reside within the Great Nation, just regular people interested in the future of this country. No fame, no glory, no interviews, no income, no expenses, and no trace of who they are. They are hoping that solutions to the causes of the impending decline of the Great Nation can be seen and implemented in time.

Best wishes.

I. M. N.

The Five Realms of Power:
An Introduction
[Paper No. 3 of the Nehemiah Papers]
I. M. Nehemiah © October 2008

The five realms of power are Governance, Economics, Religion, Justice, and Love. The realms are not necessarily equally weighted. The balances among the five realms are fluid or dynamic. A balance of powers existing at one place at one time can be different from balances found simultaneously in different places and at different times for the same place. This dynamic in balance can be impacted by outside influences, for better or for worse. Also, the five realms of power apply to situations as diverse as nations, clubs, and households, with appropriately different balances.

Each realm has several expressions. For example, the expressions of the realm of governance include democracy, theocracy, monarchy, and dictatorships. One expression of each realm is dominant in America's culture: Democracy, Capitalism, Christian Faith, Law, and Caring. Other countries might have religious dominance of governance and justice. Even at the household level in America, the expressions can easily be different from the national expressions of one or more realms, as in despotic brutal control of everything, or in faith-based sharing of resources and responsibilities. The expressions and the balances can and do vary greatly.

Each expression has one or more "currencies" which represent the most tangible and quantifiable ways to measure the amount of power in each realm.

In the following table, the realms and expressions and currencies are overly simplified for this important introductory discussion of the key concepts. Later I provide a full Paper about each of the five realms in relation to America today.

TABLE OF REALMS, EXPRESSIONS AND CURRENCIES:

Realms of Power	Expressions in America	Currencies in America	Additional Expressions and Their Currencies
Governance:	Democracy	Influence by & upon Voters	Dictatorship w/ Edicts; Theocracy
Economics:	Capitalism	Money & other capital	Socialism w/ Labor; Feudalism
Religion:	Faith: Christian	Prayers & beliefs	Non-Christian faiths, prayers & beliefs
Justice:	Law	Enforcement	Anarchy w/ Brute force; Scriptures
Love:	Caring	Service (Helpfulness)	Selfishness w/ Self-service; Hate / Jealousy

The five realms of power are out of balance in America. The imbalances have already partially crippled America and are major factors in America's current crises and impending decline. These imbalances must be addressed to avoid cumulative, accelerating damage to the nation. There is little solace in knowing that all nations throughout history have had these challenges. Indeed, as pointed out in "The Parable of a Great Nation," decline is inevitable. But decline does not need to be now in America. The key is to attain a proper balance between the five realms of power. Although this paper focuses upon America, everything I say has relevance to other nations and societies, whether rich or poor, powerful or weak, "good" or "bad," *etc.*

Multitudes of variations exist within every item in the above listing. Do not assume any black or white dichotomies. For example, capitalism in America today includes major components from socialist thought and practices. Likewise, no pure socialism exists anywhere on Earth. And there can be many corrupting influences that distort the expressions of governance, economics, religion, justice, and love. If you doubt that, just think of family relationships, whether your own or of a friend or of a character in a film or book.

Economics and Capitalism: (The second realm and its expression are discussed first because of their dominance in America.) Money is the "currency" of capitalism within the economics realm of power. And in America, the extraordinary power of money has tainted all other realms of power. Democracy in America is so overwhelmingly influenced by money that it is almost a mockery. Money in America severely impacts the legal system, many aspects of service, and even the religious fiber of our country. Therefore, several of the proposed solutions to the current crises are directly related to bringing the power of money under control. This is not an attack on capitalism and not against money. But today's capitalism and the current abusive power of money should be modified in serious ways to become "Capitalism for the Twenty-first Century," abbreviated as "Capitalism-21" or simply "C-21." (There is more about Capitalism-21 in Paper No. 5.)

◇◇

Democracy in America is based on the "currency" of votes for elected officials who then have further democratic functions.

◇◇

Governance and Democracy: Democracy in America is based on the "currency" of votes for elected officials who then have further democratic functions to propose and vote on legislation, with the elected executive branch to implement those laws. Unfortunately, America's democracy today is literally controlled by professional politicians repeatedly re-elected as "serial incumbents" who are severely influenced by money from both the left and the right. This situation is totally legal, not because it is correct or fair, but because the laws passed by serial incumbents have set the stage for this travesty of democracy under capitalist control.

Religion and Faith: Religion is the set of beliefs held by a person or society concerning the existence (or non-existence) and characteristics of some force greater than human beings, commonly referred to as "God." In general, religion fosters ethical living and promotes many concepts of kindness and fairness among people. America was founded upon beliefs in the importance of ethical living, including the teaching of such values to each generation. In this aspect, the American manifestations of "church" and "state" are united, not separated.

On the other hand, faiths (which are the practiced or functional expressions of religions) start to go their own ways, preaching their particular flavors of worship and beliefs. Beliefs are the "currencies" of religion. The various faiths represent or bestow power to their believers, giving high value to *their* "currencies" while giving very little or no value to the beliefs held by other religions. To be the chosen people of the gods (or of the one true God) is the ultimate leveraging of power. In similar fashion, some ultra-liberals have a "god" named "permissiveness" wrapped in the rhetoric of "freedom," even freedom to be offensive to others. When a person or nation believes that "God is on my side," (or "freedom justifies my imposition of permissiveness"), many deeds for good or evil are accepted and justified, especially when coupled with money and votes. Unfortunately, extremist-Americans try to make the Republicans into arch-conservative fundamentalists and the Democrats into ultra-liberal sectarians, both with their serial-incumbents as high priests. We should marginalize both extremes and concentrate on our shared core values, as found in the "reasonable person standard" that is already part of American legal traditions.

The Five Realms of Power are Out of Balance

Justice and Law: Justice is the concept that fairness should prevail. Justice is intended to be something desirable for people, but justice can be perceived in different ways. In order to minimize the conflicts over different perceptions of justice, the people in power create rules. Laws are formalized rules to govern a nation or state or city or club. There can be great laws, good laws, poor laws, and unjust laws. A law created by a designated authority is not necessarily a fair law. Powerful people make laws, in part, to maintain their view of fairness.

Laws in America too frequently tend to favor those individuals, groups, and businesses that have money and/or influence to affect voting in general elections or the subsequent actions (votes) of elected representatives. Fortunately, laws in America are forever subject to improvement, if done according to the laws about changing laws. The processes and decisions about what is and what is not allowed in America will be the ultimate battleground that will decide the future of our nation. Choose poorly and long-lasting decline will be upon us during our lifetimes. Choose wisely and greatness will continue or even expand (probably in somewhat different forms), and then future generations will take over the responsibility to preserve the nation. Proper democracy, appropriate capitalism, ethical beliefs, and a sense of caring service can combine to accomplish law-based justice to keep America on the correct path for all citizens to enjoy a more perfect union (with fairness). Be thankful that in America we still have time to choose our destiny. But it will not be easy, and it will require vast changes that impact everyone.

Love and Caring: Perhaps the truest expression of love is the caring that people are willing to give for the benefit of others. And the main currency of love and caring is service. Service can be almost synonymous with caring. Caring and service are wonderful for the personal and national psyche. They build character in men and women, young and old. There can never be too much caring or service. And yet, except for some minor efforts relative to environmental protection, almost nothing in current American capitalism (C-20) favors love and caring. Caring must be a key component in Capitalism-21.

And service can be a major ingredient in America's recipe to regain and maintain its position in World leadership, and thereby avert crisis and decline. Do not expect financially motivated corporations to seriously embrace service until either a) the shareholders demand it (by their votes or their buy/sell decisions) or b) the democratically obtained laws require or reward service efforts, especially from those persons and companies that already have an abundance of valuable skills, time, money and other assets. Service can do much to prevent the decline of America. Please note: Instead of making government responsible for needed, valued, and dutiful service, consider redirecting some of that responsibility to well-to-do people and corporations with sufficient assets to provide services. There can be motivation by sticks (taxes) or carrots (meaningful recognition of service and allowed tax deductions). America should utilize the power of love and caring through their expression as "service as a currency" to be a major alternative and balance to the power of money. I present specific proposals in later papers.

About "currencies" and their present order of importance/influence:

"Money plus other capital" is the most important and most influential of the currencies today. This includes earned money (from actual labor), growth money (from capital assets), and received money (from loans or donors such as churches, concerned persons, or organizations). Money is the most tangible and easiest to quantify on the list of currencies. Even the other forms of capital (land, stocks, owned intangibles such as patents, *etc.*) are rather easily converted into dollar values. Paper No. 5 discusses the power realm of economics.

"Influence by Voters" as expressed in election results is also very quantifiable. In a democracy, voting represents a) the concept that the people control governance via an election of legislative representatives and executive officers, and b) the concept that these elected representatives vote for specific actions. Influence by and upon voters is episodic for the pubic, occurring mainly at times of elections. But the frequent voting by elected representatives exposes them continually to pressures ("lobbies"). The ability to influence the votes of people is truly a great power, but to influence the votes of the elected representatives is even more powerful. Either way, the influence upon voting is heavily impacted by the other powers. When affected by the powers of money or beliefs, this currency of democratic power can be corrupted to become "Influence *upon* Voters," that is, the ability to influence voters (or the representatives when they vote) to deliver a desired result through their votes. Therefore, "influence" acts as a two-edged sword that must be handled with caution. Just because voting took place does not mean that true democracy has occurred. Further comments are in Paper No. 4.

◇◇◇

The ability to influence the votes of people is truly a great power, but to influence the votes of the elected representatives is even more powerful.

◇◇◇

"Prayers & beliefs" have no measurable influence outside of the person or the community of believers unless it is expressed as money or as influence over voters. The longer name for this currency is "Prayers to God and Beliefs in God," while the shorter name could be simply "God" (or "gods" to some religions). Beliefs are represented by the words and actions of members of specific faiths. There is no established "exchange rate" between different beliefs. You cannot exchange your experienced forgiveness or salvation for three purgatories, extra years on earth, or tangible assets. In contrast, you can exchange money, votes, enforcements, and service. Paper No. 6 discusses further the realm of religion and faiths.

"Enforcement of laws" for legally-defined justice is usually measured in negative or punitive terms of crime rates, arrests, convictions, prison occupancy, *etc.* It appears to be powerful, but enforcement is greatly affected by 1) variability of interpretation in the laws and 2) society's on-and-off enthusiasm for enforcement. Laws are man-made, can be rescinded or amended at any time, and are frequently ignored by the people and/or not enforced by the authorities sworn to uphold them. Law enforcement is important because laws necessarily give structure to any true changes in the power balance of the three big currencies: money, vote-influence, and God. Enforcement does the bidding of the other powers. Enforcement of culturally defined "fairness" or service is almost non-existent except to infrequently denounce or bring shame onto the unjust. (For more, see Paper No. 7.)

"**Service**" can be quantified by counting hours and/or the intensity of service work, perhaps giving some additional value relative to the effectiveness and purpose of the effort. Service inspired by the power of love and caring is mainly a personal, internal force (unless backed up by money or another of the currencies). The use of service time to impact people relative to democratic issues is inclusive in the overlap with voter influence. At present, perception of service as a currency of the power of love and caring is minimal in America compared to other currencies of power(s). As an enforceable power separated from money and influence, service lacks power for enforcement.

* * * * * * * * *

Analysis: The true importance of the five realms of power is their interrelationships, not their individual characteristics. That is why they have been introduced in one short Paper. Later, in Papers No. 4 through No. 8, I discuss each of the five realms separately in relation to America (and some aspects of the World). But in this current Paper, the interconnections and balances among the powers are the emphasis of importance. The following example illustrates this point.

In simplistic terms, socialism is based on labor as its most important "currency." That labor (drawn from everyone according to his/her abilities) somehow gets transformed into everyone receiving life's necessities (provided to everyone according to his/her needs). In a stable society, socialism has not shown advantages over capitalism, perhaps because housing, food, tickets for the bus, *etc.* are still tangible assets equivalent to "money," the currency of capitalism. Therefore, the differences between socialism and capitalism are bound up in the single realm of power called economics. Do not confuse Communist dictatorial control (governance) or atheistic practices (religion) in the former Soviet Union with economic issues of labor and capital. Soviet enforcement of laws (the realm of justice) was heavy-handed, and the realm of love/caring was very weak. In a comparison between the former Soviet Union and America today, the content and practices in the five realms are very different, but the **balance** among the five realms is surprisingly similar in that the economic realm dominates the other four realms.

So, when I speak of changing the balance among the five realms of power, I am not calling for socialism. Instead, for America, I am calling for these re-balancing efforts:

1. reduce the power of capital (by dethroning money as the measure of success),
2. redirect the power of democracy (by involving more voters and curtailing "serial incumbents"),
3. shift the emphasis within the power of faith (away from the extremes),
4. strengthen the power of law (toward compliance with laws against crime, drugs, waste, greed, *etc.*), and
5. elevate the power of caring (by providing additional meaning to life through good and meaningful service). This is where the greatest potential for change is found.

As you read the later Papers, please be aware that any single topic in isolation (such as compulsory national service for everyone) could at first appear illogical and ineffective, but becomes logical and effective when combined appropriately with other proposals. And remember that the synergy of proper combinations for balance among the five realms of power will need to be extremely powerful if we are to direct the destiny of America away from the impending decline.

Perhaps this discussion is not what you were expecting. This is not a standard "pat on the back" for America to keep going along its merry (and now failing) way. But I hope you see that my message is not one of despair but is a message with hope and prospects for solutions.

As an adult American, you have some money, you can vote, you have personal beliefs, you are subject to laws, and (I hope) you have some time for expression of love and caring through meaningful service in your life. Look upon service as a fundamental and crucial duty in your expression of love and caring for America. All five powers within your life reflect the current power relationships within America. What we should all desire are shifts for synergistic combinations of these powers so that Americans and America can understand, avoid, and even reverse the impending decline.

I see paths for hope and prosperity in our future, but not in traditional ways. I am not a prophet of doom. Instead

> *I. M. Nehemiah*
> Setting the stage for a better World

Governance and Democracy
[Paper No. 4 of the Nehemiah Papers]
I. M. Nehemiah © October 2008

The way that a nation is governed is crucial to the well-being of its people and its national identity. Democracy is widely recognized as the fairest and most desired form of governance, although it is not perfect. Monarchy, dictatorship, anarchy, theocracy, *etc.* all have even greater problems for providing long-term desirable governance.

Democracy has two primary types. 1) In a pure democracy, the people themselves govern by majority vote (at open public meetings, for example). 2) In a representative democracy (such as America), the people vote to select a set of individuals who are authorized to govern for a period of time. The elected representatives discuss and then vote; the elected executives gather information and then make executive decisions. Whether from a pure or representative democracy, we can identify three points of potential weakness in democracy.

One potential weakness is in the human nature of people. Ignorant (or biased or bribed or selfish) people could collectively decide in a pure democracy to do some rather stupid things, such as attack a neighboring nation or destroy their own economy by irresponsible government spending. Therefore, one risk in a democracy is poor judgment by a majority of the people who actually vote (even if they are a minority of the total eligible voters), and then everyone suffers the outcomes. The *Federalist Paper No. 10* describes this as control by a "faction." The saving grace in a pure democracy is that some people might know the dangers of war, over-spending, *etc*, and then convince the majority to make better choices. But they might not accomplish the correction in time to prevent permanent damage.

The second point of weakness is that the people's representatives who are selected and authorized to govern can exercise poor judgment once elected to office. Sometimes it is innocent ignorance or bias; sometimes it is intentional but legal prejudice; and sometimes it is outright dishonesty. Frequently the element of bias stems from special interest groups that heavily spend their time and money in disproportionate amounts (and sometimes illegally) to influence elected representatives. Without doubt, this can and does happen even in the best of representative democracies, and even more so in democracies weakened by centuries of biased governments or weakened by mere weeks of political propaganda or lobbying for some special purpose.

The third point of weakness is that once an unfavorable course of action has begun, it is increasingly difficult to accomplish a reversal. When a vote has decided a course of action, there is strong pressure on everyone to support the decision, especially when the stakes are high. For example, when a war is underway, even those who are against the war can be pressured (even drafted) to participate in the war efforts. And those who speak up against the actions can be labeled traitors and possibly punished. Change from established policies is usually difficult. Even in a democracy, the inertia of current practice is hard to change.

Let us never forget that some people who have been properly elected to lead have perpetrated some of the greatest evils. As one example, Adolph Hitler came to power by a democratic [process] in Germany, and his people followed him into a devastating war. Even in America, some elected persons have exploited the tremendous powers of their elected positions to perpetrate evil or some shades of gray. One example is President Andrew Jackson's actions for forced Indian removal.

Thus, democracy does not guarantee good governance. However, built into a solid democracy are established voting procedures to change laws and impeachment proceedings which can be used to remove from office officials who exercise serious misconduct or serious abuse of their power. In this Paper No. 4 we discuss some specifics of American democracy and the possible steps to improve it.

Did I just say that democracy in America needs adjustments? Yes, I did. If you agree with me or even suspect that some things need examination and possible change, please continue reading.

The "Currencies" that Impact Democracy in America

Democracy is based on the voted will of the people. And in America, the currencies of "influence," "money" and "beliefs" can strongly impact the outcomes of democratic votes. "Law enforcement" and "service" have much less impact on votes.

Have you noticed that physical power, including military power, is not on the list of powers or currencies? It did not need to be. Both a hired thug and a ballistic missile are without a conscience; it is mainly money (either directly or indirectly) and/or ideology ("beliefs") that decide their use.

◇◇

**Physical power is under the control of
the five true Realms of Power.**

◇◇

Influence by and upon Voters:

In democratic governance where "votes" are the quantified currency, the direction of government is influenced **by** voters. The ability to obtain votes in general elections or by elected representatives is extremely important. I have in mind the persuasive powers through speech and reason. These persuasive avenues are most proper where reasonable expressions of truth dominate the communications. I also think of elected chief executives (presidents and governors) who, after election, make multitudes of decisions where they cast the final (virtually only) vote because they have been empowered by the people to take action. The President of the United States has some real power.

The other side is the influence **upon** voters in order to elect persons of some specific persuasion. That is what political campaigns are all about, so certainly speeches and marketing of the candidates are appropriate, up to a reasonable limit. Our country already has some norms or limits: by law, direct bribing or buying of votes is illegal; by tradition, foul language or other immoral campaign conduct is not allowed; and by custom, the spreading of lies about candidates is considered inappropriate except when the perpetrators can get away with it, as seems to be increasingly the case.

In practice, one of the greatest one-sided advantages is to be the incumbent, the person who occupies the position and seeks re-election. This can lead to "serial incumbents" or professional politicians who occupy an elected position for many terms, even many decades. They can accomplish re-election in part because of the favors they have brought to their constituent voters. This strongly promotes actions that are short-term (until the next election) and self-serving (to gain re-election in the limited geographic area of the campaign). Re-election of incumbents does not favor long-term goals for the well-being of the nation. In times of crises such as those presently facing America, the long-term national view is far more important than the short-term local area view.

In varying degrees, all influences upon voters and their elected representatives are subject to the influence of money, which is the currency of economics and capitalism, not of governance and democracy.

Money:

American-style democracy is massively impacted by money, beginning with the episodic election process, and continuing through daily lobbying efforts. This is influence upon voters, not influence by voters.

In large measure, the veritable underlying power in American governance is the influence of money. "Money makes the World go 'round." "Money talks." Money is literally the currency of recognition and reward. A pat on the back is nice recognition, but a payment of real money is generally considered to be a deeper appreciation that can have longer lasting impacts, especially for those who are greedy or short on money. When transfers of assets are linked to governance, the results can be very unfair, whether to minorities or even to unknowing majorities in the population. Campaign money, hidden money, prospects to gain more money, lobby money, forgiveness of real and intangible debts, *etc.* are all very real factors in American elections and American politics. Not all votes and decisions are impacted by money, but far too many are.

Beliefs ("God"):

Votes and subsequent decisions by elected representatives in America can be substantially influenced by religious beliefs, including (in my definition of religion) the beliefs of the ultra-sectarians and even atheists. Strong beliefs are powerful forces, especially within the person and when expounded by leaders of groups of believers. This is neither illegal nor necessarily bad. Faith impacts politics in America. But even faiths, beliefs, and religious expression are subject to the influence of money. The examples are unending where the representatives of God in each of the faiths (including sectarianism) operate under the influence of money. Church leaders can count souls saved, attendance in church, and participants at rallies, but at the end of the day, the money the church collects from its supporters provides payment for salaries of employees (incl. leaders), attractive new buildings, utilities, insurance, and so forth.

In fairness, let's acknowledge the flow in the other direction. The perceived power of God can stimulate some persons to donate their money and time to various causes, including their preferred candidates for election. And some elected officials certainly exert their powers to favor laws or appointments of federal judges that are more in line with the thinking of the religious activists. Money talks for many in the name of God.

Discussion:

Money is closely associated with capitalism. In America, capitalism and democracy are closely linked. But, when the chips are down in America, capitalism trumps democracy, and economics is more important than governance. The people who prefer this arrangement probably have a lot of money and know how to use their money to influence the election of governance that favors their wealth or personal preferences.

I do not like that arrangement. My attitude has nothing to do with being capitalist or socialist, and nothing to do with my religious beliefs. Simply stated, governance in a democracy should not be subject to pressures for favorable treatment of wealthy people, their businesses, or their preferences. And as hard as it might be for some wealthy people to accept, in the end all true Americans would prefer revisions of capitalism to provide more strength for democratic freedom in America instead of the weakening of American democracy (and ultimately our whole society) in order to sustain and perpetuate the less desirable aspects of capitalism. I believe that.

◇◇

Governance in a democracy should not be subject to financially-induced pressures for favorable treatment of wealthy people, their businesses, or their preferences.

◇◇

Consider this textbook-style, economics-based definition of capitalism: *Capitalism is primarily based on private ownership of goods and services in a market economy in which the best business practices prevail over those that are not as good.* Now look at that same definition in relation to governance: Capitalism is primarily based on private ownership *(but "government" is not private property)* of goods and services *(but "votes" are not goods or services)* in a market economy *(but a "nation" is not simply a marketplace)* in which the best business practices *(but "democracy" is not a for-profit business)* prevail over those that are not as good *(but "fairness" is not to be prevailed over).*

I do not see how capitalism (or any economic system) has much direct relevance to democracy, and certainly no exclusive relevance to democracy. Unfortunately for America, the capitalist economic system here has shameful influence on our democratic elections through the power of money! And that money comes from the left as well as the right, from the Republicans as well as the Democrats, from the rich as well as the middle-class, but not so much from the poor.

So, how could we change things so that democracy (our system of governance) is not tainted by the most undesirable aspects of our capitalist economic system?

1. Term limits. The "serial incumbents" thrive on special-interest donations to keep them elected so they might vote in predictable ways. I write a whole section in favor of term limits in a later Paper No. 7.
2. Better controls and more balance on campaign allowances for each of up to five (?) candidates in each election, including the primary elections which decide who gets on the final ballot.

3. Development of alternatives to money as a power in politics. I am thinking of service as an alternative currency, which is discussed in other Papers. Someone who spends significant money and time to accomplish good service (in activities unrelated to politics or religion) will find more receptive listeners when speaking about politics, laws and votes.
4. Establish new laws to place the democratic processes above the reach of persons who would influence elections and decisions with money.

In short, democracy in America is too important to be left to the present system of capitalistic manipulation of voting processes. America needs to have more influence **by** voters, and less influence **upon** voters by the other powers. Power to the fair-minded voter, says

    I. M. Nehemiah
    Defender of democracy

Economics and Capitalism
[Paper No. 5 of the Nehemiah Papers]
[With an Introduction
to Captitalism-21]
I. M. Nehemiah © October 2008

Economics relates to the production, distribution and consumption of goods and services, and their management. Its diverse scope includes pork belly futures, restaurant employee labor issues, and countless other connections relative to financial matters and the management of money. Through barter or trade of currency, items of value are produced, exchanged and consumed every day, everywhere, around the World. The guiding principles and the controlling mechanisms for those economic activities vary uniquely through practice: feudalism, mercantilism, capitalism, socialism, mixed economy, *etc.* [Some pockets of old systems still exist in diverse locations on Earth.] In America, the [economic] principles and mechanisms are of capitalism. Unfortunately, the many variations of capitalism are frequently overlooked, and one variation often receives undeserved blame or credit owed to some other variation.

[Sections on Mechantilism-16 and Capitalism-17 are restructured for the 2018 publication.]

[Mercantilism-16 (approximately 1550 (mid-16th Century) to late 1600s in England, and later in other places)

Mercantilism evolved sporadically within the diversity of Feudalistic Europe with the rise of tradesmen and specialized labor. Definition: *The economic theory that trade generates wealth and is stimulated by the accumulation of profitable balances, which a government should encourage by means of protectionism.*]

[Capitalism-17 (approximately late 1600s (17th Century) to 1780s)

The earliest development of capitalism evolved in Europe, particularly in the British Isles where it was described in 1776 by Adam Smith in *The Wealth of Nations*. Smith is considered the Father of Capitalism. He also wrote *The Theory of Moral Sentiments* (1759) that states the need for sympathy and morality (caring and fair play) to achieve socially beneficial results. At this same time lived America's Founding Fathers who were certainly known for their willingness to do service to their budding nation, even at the risk of their lives. Capitalism-17 merits further study.]

[End of restructured sections.]

Capitalism-18 (approximately 17[80s] to 18[80s])

[Early capitalism continued evolving in the late 18th Century and well into the 1800s, so] I refer to it as "Capitalism-18." In Capitalism-18, free enterprise [takes hold and] allows the best to be the most successful. Let the market run freely, and society will enjoy maximum benefits. During that time, societies were mainly agricultural, while also experiencing the beginnings of [urbanization and] industrialization that grew with more factories, steamboats, railroads, stock markets and expansive banking. [In the late 19th Century after the American Civil War, industrialization and economic expansion led to the "Guilded Age" with massive fortunes of multi-millionaires.]

A published definition of capitalism speaks of an economic and social system with activities in private hands for profit, operating in a market economy to trade capital goods, labor, land and money. (Social well-being is not mentioned.) Capitalism-18 sounds good in theory. But […] people have long ago discovered that society needs to protect itself from the excesses of [unrestricted] capitalism.

In fairness, also consider the true socialism of Karl Marx. [Marx wrote in the mid-1800s amidst the English socio-economic conditions of wealth and poverty described by Charles Dickens, which is the rise of Capitalism-18.] Marx's utopian ideals based on labor and the needs of people were actually quite similar to some early Christian communities based on brotherly love. Neither was viable in the long term. Soviet communism (a form of one-party governance) was an attempt to implement socialism (an economic system). The result was anything but pure. Lenin in the 1920s was instituting financial incentives for farmers who produced more than their quotas. Communism became rife with favoritisms in housing, goods and services for those who pleased the government, making tangible benefits a variation of the monetary incentives known to capitalism. Some communist practices have been totally contrary to the principles of pure socialism.

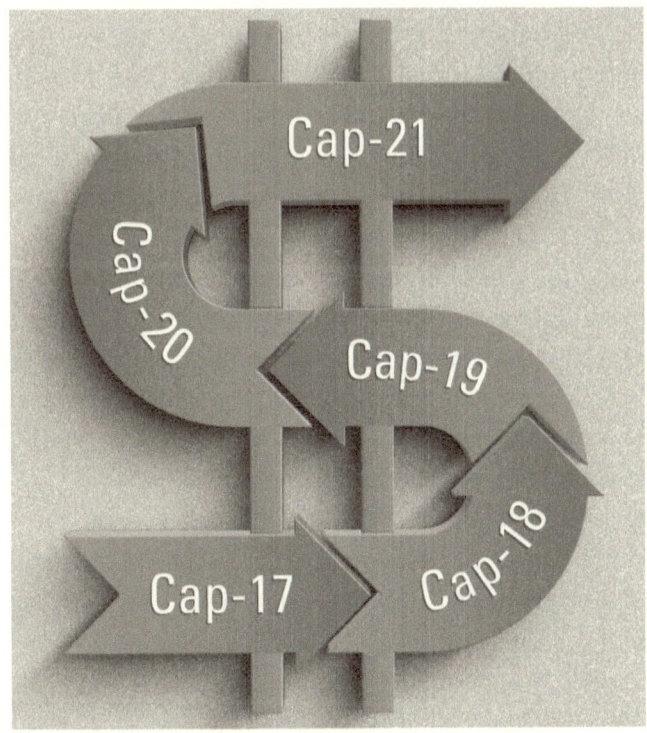

Capitalism continues to evolve.

I. M. Nehemiah

Capitalism-19 (approximately 18[80s] to 19[80])

The excessive power of industrial monopolies and banking tycoons [in Capitalism-18] caused a reaction that introduced limitations upon capitalism onward to the years before World War II. (Here called Capitalism-19). Progressive American presidents McKinley, T. Roosevelt, and Taft (all Republicans) lead the Trust-Busting efforts to prevent the largest of industries from disrupting the welfare of the American people. They created and we still have capitalist laws that give rights to laborers, whether unionized or not. Additionally, the 16th Constitutional Amendment to permit federal income taxes was ratified in 1913. The American people have spoken decisively, voting repeatedly to restrict the ravages of unbridled Capitalism-18.

Even during the Roaring Twenties, the Republican presidencies introduced additional government regulations into capitalist business practices. Unfortunately, the regulations were not sufficient to avert a national economic calamity. With the Great Depression, F. D. Roosevelt (Democrat) brought further government controls onto enterprise, banking and income. Keynesian economics with financial management (such as strengthening the Federal Reserve System influence on interest rates and creating FDIC guarantees on bank deposits) is a hallmark of Capitalism-19. Social Security was created, and Medicare came later [in the 1960s].

For centuries across Europe, America, and elsewhere, societies have placed increasing limits on capitalism. In essence, neither capitalism nor socialism has existed in a pure [unrestricted] form. There are many variations of each. Socialistic capitalism and capitalistic socialism are not so terribly far apart, especially in some European countries. In Capitalism-19, America affirmed that it is a nation governed by democratically-decided laws that can control the excessive or unbridled aspects of Capitalism-18.

After World War II, America the super-power entered [decades] of massive economic growth coupled with continued battles to relax some of the restrictions on capitalism.

[Capitalism-20 (approximately 19[80] to [present])]

[Capitalism-20 takes hold with the presidency of Ronald Reagan.] The result is Capitalism-20 in which deregulation removed many of the controls. Personal wealth accumulation has soared to deca-billionaire levels, and corporate wealth with multi-national activities has accumulated to extraordinary amounts almost beyond imagination. Today some large corporations [and even some individuals] have greater financial assets than do many nations. While our overall prosperity can be considered a great success, we are facing national challenges (including current economic crises and impending declines) that Capitalism-20 appears unable to address in appropriate and sustainable ways.

[The history or American income tax rates shows the lowering of the maximum tax rates prior to the Great Depression, the highest rates during the greatest prosperity of the 1940s through 1970s, and the major lowering that began with the Reagan administration.]

Consider 1) the historical fluctuations of the USA "Top Marginal Tax Rate" (TMT% w/ averaging of minor changes) for a married couple filing jointly, in relation to 2) the threshold of "Taxable Income Greater Than X Thousands of Dollars" (TI>$XK), above which that TMT% is applied. (Source of data: http://truthandpolitics.org/top-rates.php Comments are from I.M.N.)

Figure 5-1: Table of Top Marginal Tax Rates from 1913 to 2008

Years	TMT%	TI>$XK	Comments
1913-15	7	500K	Start of income tax in USA.
1916-17	15&67	2,000K	Two million dollars during WWI was extremely high income, so
1918-21	75	1,000K	only very wealthy people paid the highest rates.
1922-24	58&46	200-500K	Roaring 20s with great prosperity.
1925-31	25	100K	Low tax rates leading into the Great Depression.
1932-35	63	1,000K	Higher taxes to confront a national crisis.
1936-41	80	5,000K	Higher rates but very few would pay them.
1942-47	90	200K	Taxes for funding WWII, a time of national crisis.

1948-64	91	400K	Includes Truman, Eisenhower and Kennedy presidencies; 16 yrs.
1965-81	70	200K	Seventeen years without change.
1982-86	50	85K rising to 175K	Initial Reagan presidency and start of lowering tax rates.
1987	38	90K	Lower rates and lower threshold favor the wealthy.
1988-90	28	30K	Lowest tax rate since 1925-31 and the lowest threshold ever, so
1991-93	31-39	84K	more well-to-do people pay less tax than at any other time.
1994-02	39	250K rising to 307K	Most of Clinton presidency.
2003-07	35	311K rising to 350K	Fourth lowest rate since 1916.

Notes:

1. Mid-2008 instability follows 2.5 decades of great prosperity in a progressively deregulated economy with relatively low taxation of major wealth accumulation. The same period sees the national debt of 2.5 trillion dollars in 1980 double during the 1981-92 Reagan-Bush administrations, and double again to over ten trillion dollars during the 2001-2008 G.W. Bush administrations.
2. Taxes on the wealthy rise during times of national crises.
3. If adjusted for inflation, the threshold of the TMT% is extremely low since 1987.
4. Analyses of the progressive brackets and percentages of households in each bracket in key tax years might reveal more (or less) favorable treatment of upper income households today.

The above data illustrate that the highest-income earners pay far less in taxes today than did the very wealthy of even a few decades ago. This aspect of Capitalism-20 represents a throw-back past Capitalism-19 almost to Capitalism-18. In other words, the concept of progressive taxation (where the higher income earners pay higher tax rates) has been capped at only 35% for taxable income above $350,000. No wonder the high-income earners like it.

The next set of data illustrates our current [2008] rates of taxation as applied to a married couple filing jointly and having one of the following net (taxable) incomes after taking all deductions and utilizing any legal loopholes (of which there are many that favor high-income earners). Notice how much they get to keep (rounded to nearest hundred dollars). Remember, the maximum tax rate is applied only to the amount of taxable income above the threshold tied to each change of percentage. For instance, each couple keeps 90% of their first $16,650 of taxable income.

Figure 5-2: Table of Maximum Tax Rates and Resultant After-tax Income in 2008.

Taxable Income Filing jointly ($)	What they keep ($)	Max. tax (%)	Comments (Only general statements and estimations)
Zero after deductions	zero	0%	Likely negative net worth. *Also some with good incomes have many deductions and very low taxes.*
2,000	1,800	10%	Paid $200 as taxes.
5,000	4,500	10%	Many with zero savings and no health insurance.
10,000	9,000	10%	$1K paid; incl. some w/ high income but massive deductions.
16,650	15,000	10%	Lower income class (minor savings; buying house).
32,000	28,000	15%	Much of the middle class, earning $40K - $75K gross income.
63,700	54,900	15%	Very strong middle-income class (home and 401k savings).
128,500	119,200	25%	High side of middle (perhaps $100K to $500K net worth).
200,000	154,800	28%	Low side of upper income class, with substantial assets.
350,000	255,400	33%	Much is discretionary or surplus income
1,000,000	677,700	35%	every year, accumulating in capital
2,000,000	1,422,400	35%	assets of land, stocks, *etc*, with increases
5,000,000	3,188,500	35%	(or sometimes loses) in value at great
10,000,000	6,527,800	35%	growth rates but not taxed until final sale or estate taxes of up to 45%. Fortunes worth hundreds of millions or billions of dollars are created through ownership, not by hours of labor. Money makes more money for those who have it.

The above data show how Capitalism-20 "rewards" [satirical, actually works against] workers in America. There is no indication of Adam Smith's [recommended] "sympathy" by the wealthy for those in need and, likewise, for sustaining government functions. The most impressive aspect of these data is how the very wealthy are able to continue gaining wealth while the low end remains at the edge of or actually in poverty (with poor schools, unsafe neighborhoods, *etc.*), all within the wealthiest nation on Earth. America has been undergoing wealth redistribution for several decades, holding down the poor and middle class while benefiting the economically upper class.

◇◇

There is no indication in Capitalism-20 of Adam Smith's recommended "sympathy" by the wealthy for those in need and, likewise, for sustaining government functions.

◇◇

Capitalism-21 (not yet in place; proposed in 2008 and subject to modifications)

For the 21st Century, further modifications of capitalism now seem necessary. To avoid confusion among definitions, Capitalism-21 is what I. M. Nehemiah is proposing in 2008, but it might eventually be quite different in its final implementations. Or, if nothing of significance is actually implemented, Capitalism-20 will continue into the coming decades of the 21st Century with further polarization between the haves and the have-nots.

The purpose of the *Nehemiah Papers* is to help America regain strength and be prosperous in the near and distant future. I believe we need to further analyze and challenge our current capitalistic economic system (Capitalism-20) and modify it as necessary (toward the proposed Capitalism-21) for America's well-being in the coming decades. Much of our discussion relates to the role of money in determining where and with whom the power of America truly resides.

I believe money is too powerful as the overwhelming indicator of success in America, especially among well-paid professionals and business management. The poor discuss money primarily in relation to survival and getting by. The traditional middle class have enough money for the basics of life, so they discuss money in relation to modest discretionary spending, as in an occasional vacation or up-grading the family car. Those at the upper end of the middle class have been doing very well, and some, if they spend rather than save, can imitate the wealthy lifestyle. But the truly wealthy have so much money that their income and net worth define their self-perceptions of success. With money they are by definition in the higher levels of society. Wealthy people can easily attain a yearly **increase in net worth** (after their substantial lifestyle expenses and their income tax payments) that is **more than the entire gross income** of middle or lower income families.

Taxes

To pay income taxes should be considered honorable because it demonstrates the acquisition of sufficient excess income to contribute toward the operational expenses of our great country. Adam Smith was an early advocate of progressive taxation. High taxable-incomes are currently spoken of as being over $250,000 after all allowable deductions. (Personally, I would suggest $150,000 as the start of the 33% tax rate, and $300,000 to start the 50% rate.) That tax revenue should never be seen as a "loss" because the government receives it (and I do propose [and advocate] actions against waste by government). Rather, the government (if mandated) can ensure that its revenues create jobs that improve the nation (such as those in renewable energy or education or health care or law enforcement in problem neighborhoods). I prefer this to the notion that wealthy people use their excesses from reduced taxes to create jobs that may or may not relate to national needs (such as sales positions in another liquor store or another talk-show host).

Imagine a time when people proudly speak of how much they contributed to their great nation by way of their income tax. Contrast that to the current taxation system that allows legal tax avoidance wherein many wealthy persons take pride in how little in taxes they actually pay in comparison to their increase in net worth each year. Clearly, changes are appropriate.

* * * * * * *

The writings in the *Nehemiah Papers* are not an attack on capitalism or money or wealthy people. Instead, I am presenting a different perspective on capitalism and capital to illustrate our need to make some adjustments. Additional aspects of Capitalism-21 (including compulsory national service, "charter neighborhoods," and benevolent international cooperation) are detailed in the other Papers.

I sometimes wonder about great nations of the past. During the decline of the Roman Empire and the eventual collapse of Rome, did the people have any perspective on what was happening? Or did they just slip a little, and then a little more, until ruin was upon them? Did anyone tell them that their excessive domestic personal and governmental spending, their over-reaching military empire, their enslavement of the conquered (their form of economic imperialism), and their rulers' misconceptions of reality were all leading their once great nation to ruin? And, is any of that relevant to America and the World today?

If America can ignore these words, then it will ignore

I. M. Nehemiah
Challenger of the *status quo*

Religion and Faith
[Paper No. 6 of the Nehemiah Papers]
I. M. Nehemiah © November 2008

Religion may be viewed as set of beliefs of a person, a group of people, or even a whole society concerning the existence (or non-existence) and characteristics of some force or forces greater than human beings. This view therefore includes the belief that there is no such higher force, as [is the belief] in the religion of Atheism. The force or forces can be spiritual, supernatural, or some "higher-being" collectively represented by the word "god" to encompass their variety as identified in the diverse religions of the world.

With extremely few exceptions, such as voodoo and devil worship, religious beliefs accept that higher forces (that is, God or gods) are not evil or seeking to do harm to humans and the World. The perceived god can be loving, benevolent, and forgiving, but also wrathful and demanding of its believers.

In general, religion fosters ethical living and promotes some concept of being nice to other people. Therefore, I like that basis of religion because it is essentially good for human societies.

On the other hand, let us look at "faith." Faith is "practiced religion." Faiths or practiced religions (plural) typically share the common basis ("goodness") of religion described above. Within each group in isolation, uniformity of beliefs is the norm. But in their practices, individual faiths diverge on different paths, with groups preaching their particular flavor of beliefs. Differences between faiths (practiced religions) can be largely ignored as long as the religious groups are kept apart. But when there is contact and inevitable competing interests, the differences can become extremely important, even to the point of killing people. Even among Christians there are tremendous variations, with some groups mistrusting or even hating others. The same is true among Muslims. The resultant power struggles within the religious faiths are perhaps as great as the power struggles between them.

The various faiths (religions) represent power to their believers. Religion is clearly one of the five realms of power. The idea of being the chosen people of the gods (or of the one true God) is the ultimate claim of power. When a person believes that "God is on my side," many deeds for good or evil are self-justified by the holdings of religious practice. History is overflowing with examples ranging from the personal level up to the conflicts of nations.

America and the World are again faced with conditions in which the one true God has apparently selected two or more different societies as the chosen people at the same time. That is what fundamentalist Christians and fundamentalist Muslims would have us believe, but only believe their half of the story. Each "knows" they are right because God has told them so. Clearly, religion and its expressions as faiths are important for America's future.

America's Ethical Core:

Let's address the issues of religious faiths and power struggles in the context of what they mean to the future of America.

I greatly appreciate religion because it favors predictable behavior that is usually good for society and supported by laws and teachings. You generally know where you stand, even if you are a base sinner or intentionally speeding in your car. America was founded upon beliefs in ethical living and that people should be good and fair to one another. This logically includes the teaching of such values to each generation. In this aspect, the American concepts of "church and state" are united, not separated. America (the state) has never ceded to religious groups (the church) the tasks associated with maintaining an ethical and caring nation. These government tasks include lawful enforcement of decent behavior and the transmission of these reasonable standards to the entire population, reminding adults what they supposedly learned in childhood, and supporting the continuation of such teachings of propriety in public schools.

The Constitution prohibits the teaching of **specific** faith-based beliefs in public schools and public places but does not prohibit the instruction of the core values of ethical and proper living in America. BOTH the governmental "state" and the religious "church" accept (and must accept) the responsibility to keep ethical living central to American citizenry with people caring for the well-being of one another. To ignore the continuation of our core values is to invite anarchy and immorality to overwhelm us. There is no choosing between goodness and freedom. America is founded upon both, and both must be defended with appropriate vigor.

Even with the great diversity of Christian and non-Christian faiths in America, the vast majority of Americans essentially agree on the core of what is ethical and proper. We even have a legal concept called the "reasonable person standard." Granted, there are extremists in all faiths and at both ends of the liberal-conservative spectrum, and they are often the loudest voices. But they are a small component "of the people, by the people, and for the people...." The majority sets the laws.

◇◇◇

The vast majority of Americans essentially agree on the core of what is ethical and proper.

◇◇◇

Nearly all anti-church atheists do not advocate murder, theft, and total immorality. The Judeo-Christian "Ten Commandments" are nine statements of moral living and only one statement of the preference of one religion over others. (Some faiths have an eight-and-two split; see Wikipedia). Similar statements from the world's other great religions also merit public display and in-school instruction. Does a moral statement by Gandhi constitute a Hindu incursion on our society? Are Buddhist or Islamic teachings of goodness to be ignored because of their origins? Clearly not.

Then why are they not on display? Because nobody bothered to put them up, knowing that the displays and teachings most understood and accepted in America are those of the Judeo-Christian tradition. So, let us display additional ones while not taking down traditional ones that remain good and useful. Reminding people of their core values is important to maintain America on the track of proper and decent living. Reminding adults and teaching children about America's core values are as important for American morals as singing the National Anthem and saying the Pledge of Allegiance are for patriotism. Patriotism, decent morals, and a sense of fair play are not policies or laws; they are the bases upon which the American people should create their policies and laws.

Two brief examples: "Thou shalt not kill" does not resolve the legal question concerning the point at which a fertilized egg or fetus constitutes human life. And "Thou shalt not steal" does not cover all aspects of how people with corporate and personal greed can take advantage of other people but escape consequences via loopholes and astute lawyers. But killing and stealing are inherently wrong and we should instruct our next generations about decent and important core values. In a democracy, laws are (or should be) based on the core values of the people, and if those values are weak or absent, the society will suffer accordingly, even leading to disastrous decline.

The Judeo-Christian-Muslim Traditions

America is by far a Judeo-Christian country by historical traditions and current practices. I once thought that the "Judeo-" word referred to the modern-day Jewish community in America. [The Jewish population is an important segment of America noted for their financial success and political influence, but is only two-percent of the American population.] No, "Judeo-" really refers to the historical background of Christians before Jesus, as in the Old Testament part of the Bible. That is an important link if Christians are to believe that they are the chosen people of God. The link to God is via Adam and Eve to Abraham and his son Isaac to Jacob and the Twelve Tribes of Israel, and onward to King David and his descendents Mary and Joseph and to Jesus, the starting point of the Christian half of the name "Judeo-Christian."

Many Americans also know but have forgotten that Islam also traces its roots back to the Garden of Eden. Abraham actually had two sons. The Bible tells us about Ishmael, son of Abraham and Hagar. The Islamic link back to God is via Ishmael, the first-born son of Abraham, instead of via Isaac. So, quite literally the Jews, Christians, and Muslims are all really brothers and sisters in *one* family under their *one* true God.

In my youth I fought with my brothers and sisters. Some were real tussles that Mom and Dad had to break up. I did not fight nearly as much with my classmates at school, not even the ones who were far worse than my siblings. Why? Because proximity creates conflicts. Not just the physical proximity of sharing the same television set, but cultural proximity of competing for parental attention.

And so it is with religions, especially those that branch off from the same roots and trunk. The old faith versus the new faith is a classic tale. Always the new faith accepts the basics of the old faith (otherwise the new would have cut off its own roots). And the new faith always claims that it has something more, something better, and something closer to the deities. But the keepers of the old faith describe the new folks with words like heretic and blasphemer and misguided soul. The resultant troubles can include killings and holy wars. Such problems flare up occasionally, depending on proximity, firebrand leaders, changes in population percentages, challenges to territorial influence, and some bad luck.

So Catholics and Protestants [harm] each other in Northern Ireland; Sunnis and Shiites hate each other in the Middle East; Hindus and Muslims clash in the India/Pakistan region; and Jews and Muslims fight military battles and conduct terrorism around Israel. All of those conflicts are within recent years, and many persist to this very day. Go back a few decades or centuries and we find the Spanish Inquisition, the Crusades, the Islamic invasion of Europe up to Vienna, the persecutions of Sikhs and Baha'i and Mormons, Branch Davidians, and other "Holy Interventions." And the ancient civilizations of Romans, Assyrians, Mongols, Aztecs, *etc.* fought as believers in their gods, with a hearty mix of political empire building to stoke the fires.

And EACH OF THEM said that gods or God was on their side.

To that I say "nonsense"! I could not maintain my belief in God if I thought God was so fickle as to play with his various "chosen people" as can be seen in history.

I can believe (and I want to believe) in a supernatural power greater than anything human because I want life to be better for myself and all other people. That belief helps me remain sane, even when the world societies around me seem so insanely and narrowly mal-focused about hurting each other or not caring about others. I will repeat that in different words: There are outwardly religious people in America (and elsewhere) who are proclaiming their faiths but who do not show true sincere caring for other people, even those close to them.

◇◇

There is nothing, absolutely nothing, to indicate that America is any more or less chosen by God than is or was any other nation or society today or throughout history.

◇◇

What does this discussion have to do with Building a Better America and a Better World? Everything! America cannot avoid its probable decline unless it alters its attitudes and actions. There is nothing, absolutely nothing, to indicate that America is any more or less chosen by God than is or was any other nation or society today or throughout history.

So, whether or not you believe that America is favored by God, if America wants to avoid its impending decline, we citizens must act now to do a better job at being nice people at home and in the World. We need other nations to genuinely like us and even love us. And surely your God, however you define him/her/it, would want you to help make that happen.

The Currency of Religion and Faith is Prayers and Beliefs

Prayers and beliefs (and we can include miracles) are of extremely high value, but only to the believers. That currency has little or no value to others. As an analogy, consider a "money exchange" office that accepts only one type of money (such as dollars or Euros or yen) and has no exchange rate with other currencies. Literally, there would be no transactions. And so it is with the currencies (prayers, *etc.*) of different religions. Therefore, the currencies of religions and faiths are traded within the confines of each religion itself. Do not count on the highly intangible faith-based currencies of religion to alter the balances among the Five Realms of Power.

However, religion has an established history of impacting the other Realms of Power by utilizing its influence with the other four currencies:

1. Economics: some faiths have immense amounts of money and physical assets.
2. Governance: religion can "bring out the vote" when requested, including placing religious leaders into key positions.
3. Religion: great power among the faithful believers, but little power among the non-believers.
4. Justice: the dominant religion frequently impacts the laws of the land, even to instances where Biblical Law or Islamic Law or theocracy (governance by god) has absolute legal powers.
5. Love: churches can deliver enormous amounts of service, including the non-sectarian services of fund raising, preferences of political candidates, promotion of patriotism, advocacy of ethical/moral living according to the laws, and "love thy neighbor as thyself."

Ironically, religion can have sufficient impact via ***non-faith*** currencies to alter the course of history, even to prevent the decline of great nations. How religion impacts the prospects for Capitalism-21 and the future of America remains to be seen.

Some Concluding Thoughts

1. Your faith is special to you, not to others.
   A. (Mainly for radical Christians and the far right wing): Stop injecting your "holiness" into the lives of others. It is downright irritating and can reveal your hypocrisy. You are forcing your religious values as if you were the "owners" of ethical and proper conduct, thereby bringing the church into such domains as our public classrooms, which is unlawful. Instead, ethical and proper conduct and decency are AMERICAN values (meaning they are "state" values) that you can actively advocate for our schools (without trying to make this a religious or faith-based issue).

B. (Mainly for Atheists and the far left wing): Stop preaching your standards of "modern" (as in "weak") morality and hiding behind some warped sense of "freedoms" that you manipulate to promote your form of "faith." Lead your lives as you choose, but do not advocate your "holiness" into the lives of others.

C. (All the rest of you): Yes, this does apply to you and me. Stand up for decency and order and justice as American ethical values, but without the trappings of religions. Some of us need to start or strengthen those values inside our own homes and neighborhoods. And if association with churches and genuinely good people will help you, seek them soon.

2. LIVE your faith. I mean [live] the good [proper] life-style part, not the preachy part. Others might see your good deeds, but you do not need to tell them or make a show of your goodness. Just do it. Encourage others to help.

3. Direct the resources of your faith toward the betterment of life for others. What community uses exist for that nice church building or property? How much of your donations and offerings to your faith are doing good for others and good for America? Be sure to exclude the expenditures for "preaching the faith" and for self-serving property (buildings, buses, land, fuel, utilities, *etc.*) and social functions. How much are you doing with your church resources to help build a better America and a better World?

4. Actually reach out to members of other faiths and seriously be their friends, not just be near them to preach the benefits of joining your congregation. Honestly try to understand their faith or lack of faith. You might learn something about your own faith in the process and, who knows, some people very different from you might join (and alter?) your congregation.

5. And do all of the above internationally as well as in America. Earnestly direct significant resources to those impoverished overseas areas irrespective of their beliefs.

Please do not call me a church basher. Who knows, I might attend church more regularly than you do. In fact, I might be that person in the next pew who is fervently praying while you are looking around. You don't know me, except that

    I. M. Nehemiah
    A believer in goodness

Justice and Law
[Paper No. 7 of the Nehemiah Papers]
I. M. Nehemiah © November 2008

Justice is the concept that fairness should prevail. People inherently desire justice. But all too often, justice is practiced as retaliation. Criminals get sent to jail; evil people go to hell; and the poor try to take wealth from the rich. Even the expression "our turn will come" reflects the belief that one's share of power, money, prestige or anything "owed" is being (unjustly?) denied. Frequently, justice is in the eye of the beholder. And when the beholder's eye is biased or limited or even totally blind, injustice can prevail.

Therefore, to minimize the cases of conflict over perceived justice, the people in power establish rules. In the olden times of monarchies, kings had the power to determine the definition of justice, often with questionable results. In modern times, dictators have taken the place of kings. In democracies both old and recent, the people or their selected representatives establish a set of laws and a cadre of judges to oversee compliance with those laws.

Laws are formalized rules to govern defined associations of people, typically a nation or state or city or club. America often expounds proudly on its governance by laws. Certainly, reasonable laws are much better than arbitrary *ad hoc* judgments. But there can be great laws, good laws, poor laws, outdated (or irrelevant) laws, and unjust laws. The authority of a body to create a law does not necessarily assure the fairness of that law. For example, England under rule of King George III made a perfectly legal law about taxation on tea to the British colonies. Some citizens willfully broke that law, and we celebrate their actions. Furthermore, the wonderful Constitution of the United States of America was so imperfect that amendments were eventually needed to allow women and Afro-Americans and even the Native Americans the right to vote in their own country. Nelson Mandela spent 27 years in prison for breaking legally enacted laws under Apartheid in South Africa. Powerful people make laws, and it is only natural (but not necessarily fair) that their laws help maintain their view of what is to be allowed.

In today's America, we have laws (or a lack of laws) about taxes, registration for military service, environmental protection, labor relations, marriages of same-sex partners, and on and on and on. We generally applaud our laws and keep most of them. However, the best thing about laws in America is that its citizens can undertake actions to change any law by adhering to laws for changing laws (which can also be changed). Yes, America is a nation governed by laws, but there is no law that any law cannot be changed lawfully. That is not double talk. It is the only way that America can truly improve itself with fairness as defined by law.

The Currency of Justice and Law is Enforcement

The term "enforcement" brings to mind police officers. Yes, they are important and are generally fair-minded. And of course there are issues of lack of enforcement for a multitude of reasons, including neglect in some troubled neighborhoods (discussed in later Papers). However, for our discussion of the balances among the Five Realms of Power, it is the long-established "system" of enforcement that is more crucial for America than are the individualized enforcers.

Justice is good, but it implies that somebody is a judge or a jury member. Fortunately, laws are made to guide judges and juries in making correct decisions. Unfortunately, both judges and laws are subject to the influence of other powers and forces. And in America, the highest power has frequently been the money of capitalism, and the second highest power has been the government by elected representatives. Forget about the power of faith and prior law and love. Our justice system is severely contorted by the power of money and elected officials. And there lies the problem of justice in America. Money influences elections, and elected representatives make laws that favor those with money.

Do not misunderstand me. I did not say that America is unjust. I love America, in part because we have one of the best countries on Earth in terms of justice. Equal justice for all, under the law. And what is the law? The law provides that anyone can have his or her day in court to present his or her case. That part of American justice is most admirable.

But a day in court does not always result in a satisfactory decision. Perhaps a law is antiquated and imperfect. Perhaps the other side also had a very good point and so a compromise judgment resulted. Perhaps some important evidence was not available (or intentionally withheld by the opposition). Perhaps unusual pressures unrelated to the proceedings affected the judge's mental state. Perhaps the opposition had some undisclosed or unfair or purchased (but not illegal) advantage, such as a masterful and eloquent lawyer. Perhaps something illegal such as jury tampering or bribing the judge was done but not detected. You have had your day in court. But did you get true justice? Most of the time, you probably did. But sometimes, what was legal justice is not actually just or fair or right.

◇◇

Money influences elections, and elected representatives can and do make laws that favor those with money.

◇◇

Let's go back to the problem that "Money influences elections, and elected representatives [can and do] make laws that favor those with money." Because America is essentially a capitalistic nation (with some social moderation as discussed previously), it is logical and appropriate that there are laws that stimulate business and labor and agriculture and science. But there can be many "variations" of such laws. As we might say, "The devil is in the details." Tax cuts or tax increases can disproportionately favor some more than others. Expenditures such as subsidies can favor some more than others. Permissions or denials for actions can favor some more than others. And it is human nature to want to be among the favored. To "want" is basically passive; to "facilitate" or plead or pressure or bribe or threaten is much more active. Activists, also known as lobbyists, are abundant in the realms of American government at all levels. And activist action can certainly bring more results than passive wanting and waiting.

Limiting the influence by lobbyists is a political topic in 2008 and earlier. Let's make sure that tough controls are in place and monitored. I have nothing against lobbying in principle, but much against its oft-unfair practice.

Term Limits

Democracy is wonderful, but not perfect. Perhaps the most serious problem with democracy is its notorious shortsightedness, meaning vision only as far away as the next election. Democratically elected leaders often lack (or will not use) long-term vision necessary for sustained resolve for needed actions. To stay in power, that is, to be re-elected, overshadows concerns that are beyond the next election.

The weakening (and possible destruction) of a true democracy can come from the excessive power of professional politicians, also known as serial-incumbents. [Sort of like serial killers, serial-incumbents do their deed over and over again.] These people are elected time after time after time, which is their primary objective. Their actions during their elected terms are notably influenced by how each action will impact their re-election. And they respond in large measure to those who most help them get re-elected through the powers of money or influence upon voters in their electoral niche.

Abraham Lincoln was an experienced lawyer, an elected representative in Illinois state government, a *one*-term Illinois representative to the US Congress (meaning two years in Washington), and defeated in his bid to become a US senator. Those were his formal credentials prior to being elected President of the United States of America in 1860. He was never the chief executive of any state or significant business. And yet he exercised his duties in office and became a highly esteemed President. The quality of the person can be more important than the experience.

On the other hand, various US Presidents rose from the ranks of serial-incumbents. Several were very effective; several were quite poor at the job. Numerous were brought to power via established sources of money and influence. Their elections were little more than astute political ventures executed as games of strategy and power.

Politics is the process by which two or more people make decisions that affect anything, including themselves. Politics involves negotiation, compromise, deal making, and decision making. We hope political processes engender good values and proper conduct, but that is neither obligatory nor part of the definition.

A person elected to political office has power. He or she is granted power to represent the people (constituents) who elected him (or her). And power attracts additional powers. People with money and/or influence soon determine whether an elected person already favors or can have their favor affected sufficiently to [vote in accordance] with a desired point of view. If favored votes are forthcoming, the elected person has influential support to assist in re-election. Therefore, an incumbent has improved chances to be serially elected. Fifteen elections means thirty years in the US House of Representatives, and a few persons have exceeded that. The serial-incumbents are professional representatives of whatever forces can bring them re-election. I did not say they were representatives of their constituents. They only need their own vote plus fifty percent of those voters who bother to show up on their day of (re-)election.

Imagine an election without any incumbents. A clean slate. A fresh start. The fresh candidates will have already attracted supporters during the campaign, including those with money and the ability to influence. But the candidates cannot utilize an incumbent's powers. I like that idea. Here are a few reasons [in favor of] term limits, plus comments in response. I use the US House of Representatives as an example.

1. *Incumbents have experience in the workings of the House.* By "workings" do you mean the basic functioning or the deal-making? Basic functions can be learned quickly. Deal-making has connotations that are at least as bad as they might be possibly good.
2. *Incumbents represent their congressional districts better.* Elected persons spend more time in Washington than in their home districts. Certainly a fresh person from that same district knows the current needs and desires of those people as well as an incumbent, especially of an incumbent who has additional interests brought to them by lobbyists and other one-sided influences. Seven US States have only one representative, and the average population

per Congressional District is 646,946 persons, so having representatives that come from different towns in the District might yield better representation.

3. *Incumbents know how to bring benefits to their home districts.* If that includes the generally shameful earmarks and pork-barrel appropriations that get tacked onto legislation, then keep the incumbents out of office! Earmark projects basically "buy" votes using Federal funds to get employment or other benefits for the home district. Such projects should be closely evaluated in terms of national interests, not just slipped in under the cover of other (presumably desired) legislation. There seems to be a marketplace of earmarks in Congress where "I'll vote for your earmark in exchange for your vote for mine or for some other favor." Or is it "I won't reveal your agenda if you don't reveal mine." Imagine that! Serial legislators can sell (actually trade) their votes in Congress to obtain help to get re-elected. The elimination of earmarks and pork-barrel legislation would save substantial amounts of money for better use elsewhere.

I have not said that an elected person cannot be elected again. I just said he or she should not be allowed to be elected **to the same position** in continuous sequence. Therefore, after a two-year term and a two-year break, the person could seek the same position. Also, an out-going US Representative could seek election to the US Senate, and then return for election to the House two years later if he/she lost, or six years later if victorious for the Senate. Or the Congressional Representative could run for election as a state representative or state senator or even as a state governor. That would result in a substantially larger pool of people with experience in government and far fewer "obligations" to lobbyists and other purveyors of influence.

◇◇◇

Prohibit serial incumbents. Allow only <u>one</u> sequential term in the same position for national and state offices.

◇◇◇

We could even think of elected positions as being akin to "service missions" for two years. That might attract more candidates who take a break from being a corporate manager, or a parish minister/priest/rabbi, or a labor organizer, or a school teacher/professor, or a lawyer such as Lincoln. And if they are notably effective at the job of representative governance, they could consider a six-year term as a Senator. But six years in the Senate would be enough. Go back to private life, or run again for the House, or try to be mayor of your town.

Term limits. Yes. Only *one* term in sequence for national and state offices. And that applies to the US presidency also. If the person's service in office is favorably memorable, he or she should have an excellent chance to be elected again after waiting one electoral cycle. And if the Vice President performs well, he or she should be able to carry on the work of the President who is leaving office. Consider this: One term in office is enough time to do some good, but not enough time to do permanent damage (we hope). Consider our recent Presidents with second terms: Johnson (Vietnam); Nixon (Watergate); Reagan (Iran-Contra); Clinton (Lying under Oath); and G. W. Bush (Iraq). A sequence of different people who can act for the **long-term** well-being of America is needed. It is desperately needed, without delay.

In any election, we will never have perfect candidates. People are not perfect. America survives with the ups and downs of the quality of its Presidents, senators, representatives, and state/local officials. That is life and quite natural. What should be avoided is the serial occupancy of any elected position. New blood is needed at each election. And the ability of special interest groups with money and influence to manipulate favors from serial-incumbents would be thankfully curtailed.

When opponents to these proposed strict term limits start to appear, be sure to check on their past records to see if and how serial-incumbents have provided them with benefits. Expect strong resistance from the serial-incumbents themselves. Expose them and remove them. When America can improve its democracy, then it can govern itself better and also show other democracies how to get fresh representation that is not tainted by long-standing special interest groups. After all, we are speaking of avoiding the decline of America and the World.

This essay is about justice and law. Term limits brings better justice. And term limits are as easy to accomplish as the changing of election law. Easier said than done, yes. But something that should be done for the well-being of America. Indeed, I am biased against the overly powerful special interest groups and the excessive impact of big money. But after all is said and done, I am seeking to build a Better America and a Better World. Why? Because

> *I. M. Nehemiah*
> Advocate for justice and law

Love and Caring
[Paper No. 8 of the Nehemiah Papers]
I. M. Nehemiah © November 2008

Note to Readers: Love is the fifth "realm of power," and in earlier Papers I used the word "service" for both the expression and currency of Love. Now I have changed the "expression" from service to "caring." The word "service" is still the correct term for the "currency" of love and caring. This wording change will eventually be made in Papers No. 1 and No. 3.

Love is a strange concept to be called the fifth realm of power. One dictionary definition calls it "intense affection." Its expression is something like "beneficent caring." But what is beneficent to one might be an anathema to someone else. Either way, love is an extremely powerful force. In a popular novel, Lord Voldemort forgot that a mother's love for her son, Harry Potter, was a powerful form of old magic. In a different form, love for a country can motivate a soldier to do heroic deeds on the battlefield, some so remarkable as to merit posthumous receipt of the Congressional Medal of Honor. Yet, in its complexity, love of one's religion can motivate a suicide bomber. Do not underestimate the power of love.

The "currency" of love is "service," the quantifiable and observable acts that people do for the benefit of others. Service for the benefit of others is among the most charitable forms of love. America needs love, and America needs service. America tends to underscore its focus on acts of kindness around "special holidays" such as Thanksgiving and Christmas when such stories frequently are promoted in the media as "feel good" events. Service, whether holiday-inspired or year-round, is wonderful for the personal and national psyche. But is there enough of it? Can there ever be too much service? Can love, caring, and service be part of the way for America to regain and maintain its position in World leadership? Can service be a sign of weakness or arrogance? We will discuss the possible roles of love, caring and service in relation to America's attempts to delay the absolute truth of the decline of all previous prosperous and powerful nations.

In comparison with many other nations, America is already a leader in volunteer service. Our students are often encouraged to volunteer to help in whatever ways they are best able. Service has become an item for applications to universities and on employment resumes. Employers frequently look for prior service as an indication of a well-rounded person who is not self-centered. Churches, clubs, and informal groups provide thousands of hours of unpaid service for the well-being of others.

The above paragraph is a "feel good" statement. I have no complaints about it, but I do offer some observations and suggestions in the light of avoiding a decline in America.

1. America would benefit from a massive increase in levels of caring and service.
2. Many more Americans need to be involved in that increase in caring and service.
3. We must analyze and adjust where and to whom caring and service are best directed.

How Service can help

Progress implies accomplishing something favorable, often in materialistic or social terms. We often measure progress in monetary terms such as increased gross domestic product, rising stock market values, increased net worth of an individual or corporation, buying a new car or larger home, *etc.* On the social side, we check on improvement of test scores in schools, indices of health, and lower crime rates. Those social examples are generally associated with the effects of labor, such as in law enforcement, medical care, teaching/education, management, sales, or good investment efforts. Paid or unpaid, that work is a form of service. Thus we start to observe that both money and social service can be used to measure the status of a person or nation.

For a moment, imagine how an unpaid [or low-paid] volunteer could accomplish those social improvements. Okay, assume that the volunteer actually has some relevant credentials or supervised training to do the job either paid or un-paid. Volunteer tutoring of children in schools or in evenings requires some education, but not a university degree and teacher's certificate. Volunteer neighborhood watch, especially in a troubled neighborhood, adds eyes and ears to our police force. People doing something good for others can contribute to our national well-being.

Obligatory National Service

Nationally organized service to the nation is already an established practice in America and many other nations. Most widely practiced is military service. America today has only a voluntary military service that is based on attractive payments and incentives for enlistment in the armed forces, including the National Guard. The call of patriotism is clearly an incentive for enlistment, especially in times of war. In previous wars, compulsory military service was standard practice and acceptable to the American public and their elected representatives.

Apart from middle-aged individuals who chose a career in the military, national service has been almost exclusively for young adults ages 18 through 30 years old. The Peace Corps and the AmeriCorps are non-military examples of excellent service opportunities already in operation. The amount of good that could be accomplished by millions of additional service-days could have a very beneficial impact on America and the rest of the World.

◇◇◇

Al̲l̲ Americans and legal residents should be required to do national service appropriate to their circumstances.

◇◇◇

Most Americans have never done any national service. For America to avoid the impending decline, I propose that *all* adult Americans be required to serve this nation. Yes, I am referring to both men and women, and to all adult age brackets. Such service could be in many forms. Here are a few notes:

1. Every adult American from 16 to 75 years of age should be registered and evaluated for National Service, with recognitions and some exceptions given for those who have already performed some acknowledged form of [significant] service. No exemptions would be pre-recognized, not even for health causes unless extreme, such as total mental incompetence, missing three or more limbs, or physically attached to medical equipment that conflicts with every form of service opportunity. For example, persons with asthma but still able to speak normally might serve as readers to blind persons or be observers at suspected trouble spots.

2. Acknowledged forms of prior or on-going service include active military duty, cumulative time of active duty in the National Guard and Peace Corps, school teaching in identified problem areas such as ghetto schools, and accumulated time in yet-to-be-recognized service missions (excluding faith-promoting missions).

3. A lifetime cumulative period of two years is considered to be the minimum service time in the initial implementation of this plan. Considering 50 weeks per year and 40 working hours per week, 2,000 working hours per year (4,000 total) would be the absolute minimum for required National Service. Later it might be raised to be 10% of the adult lifetime of each American. For example, a 48-year old person would be expected to have contributed three years of national service during his or her first thirty adult years.

4. For young adults, paramilitary training and service would be required as part of the two-year obligation. Between ages 18 and 22, every able-bodied young adult [both male and female] would complete at least six-months total (perhaps 3 two-month periods) of full-time active duty including the equivalent of basic training and further service activities under military-style administration. The ability of America to defend itself is enhanced when more and eventually all Americans have had basic military training. American self-discipline is enhanced with the rigors of basic training and

discipline. Freedom is not free. [Conscientious objectors do not fire weapons but do have the other training and service tasks.]

5. America wants tough and important jobs done, and some would require the organizational skills of the military or Peace Corps. Many young adults would be part of the expanded paramilitary forces responsible for certain major international assistance tasks, such as constructing infrastructure and/or providing development training as appropriate to cooperating nations. Others will be part of a highly expanded (perhaps 100 times larger) Peace Corps more focused on appropriate and sustainable enhancement to the lives of impoverished people overseas. As much as possible, each person's training and abilities will be utilized; [this provides] valuable experience not only to recent college graduates, but [to] all citizens entering or re-entering the workforce. Moreover, those who do not go to college will learn job skills in the military while doing three or four years of enlistment, as currently done, but with less military and more civil-development emphasis.

6. As in the current operations of the Peace Corps and military service, active members are paid. But payment beyond food and housing would be minimal and according to need for accomplishing the task. Able-bodied men and women would not be allowed to select easy tasks close to home. Persons who do serve close to home in their spare time would serve extra years and probably receive no payment except the honorable notification of accomplishment and fulfillment of duty. On the other hand, a person serving full time away from home might even receive a hardship bonus depending on the task.

7. Additional service hours could be counted in the time requirements that must be fulfilled by people on the revised welfare system in America. There will be no "free lunch." The welfare system would be much less of an unsupervised handout and much more of a semi-personalized assistance plan with regular supervision. The welfare recipients would be required to participate in appropriate programs. Some program supervision would be by compulsory national service personnel. Other service will be by one welfare recipient who assists another recipient with a different set of problems. All of this

involves people and the management of people. And that means job creation of all types. And these are not jobs that could be outsourced overseas. These are American jobs to assist other Americans, bringing dignity even within the [revised] welfare system.

8. Persons over the age of 50 could be allowed to make a payment in relation to their net worth and/or gross income that would equal no less than what they would have earned in two years of employment at the highest level of their earning power. No deductions or exemptions would be recognized, not even for taxes paid. No exceptions. Put in the money or put in the time. It could be quite honorable for a highly-paid person to remain in his or her position of financial earning-capacity and accumulate extra years of service via such payments. Consider the multi-million dollar per year executives and celebrities who could serve well by donating the value of a year of their [gross] income once every five years.

9. A very large proportion (perhaps seventy-five percent of the total service) would be directed internationally. This national service performed overseas would be in cooperation with agreeing nations, as in the expanded Peace Corps and other development programs. See Paper No. 16 about "charter nations" and international service.

10. With such a massive increase in national service positions, the American economy would benefit from reduced levels of unemployment as well as the accomplishment of many important tasks that have been neglected in recent decades. The economy is stimulated by service. Service is honorable and commendable. The elevation of service as an important "currency" in America is crucial to the implementation of Capitalism-21.

The American people, via their elected representatives, have the power to enact laws that would require all Americans to provide some form of national service. Unfortunately a nation stagnant in its self-indulgence (as is America) is unlikely to implement such actions. Our hope is that the realization of the impending serious decline of America will shake the core of our society and generate the desire to implement these proposals along with other necessary changes.

Service as a Currency to Help Balance the Power of Money

In several Papers, I write about the excessive power of money (or the lack it) to impact our democracy and our life-styles. Now, when financial difficulties face our country, we talk even more about money. We fear the loss of jobs and economic recession, where people have less purchasing power and buy less (either because they do not have the money to spend or they shop wisely to save money). But that spending decline causes even more job losses, causing leadership to provide stimulus packages that encourage more spending. This is an apparent contradiction that needs analysis. The root of the problem concerns *what* is purchased. Americans must spend less on the unnecessary and spend more, much more, on the truly necessary. Some experts point out the need to "spend" our way out of a recession or depression, and such must be done wisely.

The unnecessary: Prosperous America was attacked on 9-11-2001. Part of President G. W. Bush's response was to encourage Americans to be normal and to go out and spend. There was no tightening of belts or encouragement of spending in the direction favoring important necessities. And the people did spend on many, many unnecessary items. We need to be mindful of the difference between functional clothes vs. fashionable clothes, home-cooked nutritious food vs. fancy restaurants and fast-foods, high MPG vehicles vs. SUVs, adequate housing vs. extravagant homes, interesting vacations vs. luxurious travels, competent legislation vs. pork-barrel projects, savings vs. credit-card debt, *etc.* Note that most of this unnecessary spending is related to personal satisfaction under the control of individuals acquiring benefits for themselves; [it is] not from government programs. That may bring some solace from the vantage of the taxpayer, but the problem of unnecessary spending did not start in 2001. It has been creeping into America for many decades. And the same problem occurred in earlier great nations, all of which have fallen from their positions of tremendous power. The self-indulgences of Roman leaders and citizens are legendary and led to their eventual weakness; someday the self-indulgences in America under Capitalism-20 may be similarly viewed as foreshadowing our decline.

The necessary: If we had spent less lavishly we should have had some funds for the important tasks of better schooling, safer neighborhoods, larger Peace Corps, social programs with more human interaction and less hand-outs, improved mass transit, infrastructure maintenance, adequate (not lavish) health care for all citizens, and even perhaps a close-to-balanced budget. Please note that almost everything listed as necessary is strongly related to some form of governmental control or sponsorship (IF the government acts responsibly instead of wastefully). Do not expect the wealthy to provide these necessities in their unprompted course of goodwill. They are too busy leading the way to conspicuous consumption.

Recently I heard a news commentator say that in these financially-constricting times we should lower taxes on the lower and middle classes so they would have more money to spend. I agree and add that within the lower economic classes, a greater percentage of their money would be (or at least should be) spent on necessities, including debt reduction. Concerning the wealthy, the commentator advised postponing any increases in taxes on the wealthy because that would restrict their spending. Certainly with higher taxes they would have less money to spend, but to spend it on what? They spend firstly on themselves choosing the lavish and unnecessary (the mansions and SUVs and fancy stuff), and proportionately little on the "necessary" components named above.

⟨⟨⟩⟩

Promote and encourage the fountains of wealth in America to stream their money into the "necessary" categories of spending.

⟨⟨⟩⟩

This leads to **a key point in Capitalism-21: Promote and encourage the fountains of wealth in America to stream their money into the "necessary" categories of spending.** Some multi-billionaires are already started on that road (*e.g.,* Gates, Buffet, Bloomberg), and they are not suffering in their life-styles. Others should share generously also. And if they do not, then our laws should be changed to provide for them increased incentive to do more service with their money. How? By adopting a tax structure that rewards service through donations and sponsorships to approved activities of national benefit.

For example, if a person earns more that five million dollars (gross income with few deductions allowed), then 80% of the amount over five million can be given tax free to acceptable (approved) activities for the benefit of the nation. Assume that a sports star or TV personality earns $10 million per year. The extra five million would generate $4 million for approved projects, and the person still keeps one million dollars. Perhaps the $4 million would be for scholarships and grants for improved schools or security in a challenged neighborhood near the professional athlete's sports stadium, or to promote investigative news reporting by students (sponsored but not controlled by news commentators), or assistance to activist groups concerning the environment or drug dealing or other issues that should be exposed and corrected. We would all cheer for that wealthy person who is doing so much good with his or her money. And if he or she declined to do that service, then the $4 million would be collected as income tax revenue, and then the government could try to improve schools and security, *etc.*

* * * * * * * * *

I hope you understand these basic ideas about accomplishing more service through time-on-task and through money-directed-for-service. All people, whether rich or poor, need to break away from the distorting influences of money and self-serving indulgences. We need to start using our money and our time in the service of our nation. I revisit this subject in later Papers to give more details and examples.

* * * * * * * * *

This concludes the five essays on the Five Realms of Power (Papers 4 through 8). The realms of power are out of balance in America. Capitalism-21 is introduced as a way to restore the needed balances. In particular, the currency of service must be strengthened, and the currency of money brought under appropriate control. Perhaps these rather unusual and challenging proposals might not be agreeable to you. But I hope you will be supportive of the need for discussion. What is important is whether or not the proposals would be good for America and for the World. America must discuss and decide (or face the consequences of inaction). I believe our current realities and proposed solutions as outlined in the next two Papers direct us to alter the course of America's destiny. YOU must discuss and act. I have only the single voice of

> *I. M. Nehemiah*
> An American volunteer for service

The Nehemiah Postulates
[Paper No. 9 of the Nehemiah Papers]
I. M. Nehemiah © November 2008

A "postulate" (noun) is a statement that someone claims to be true and upon which further discussion is based. The fifteen Nehemiah Postulates are summary statements upon which the prior and further writings are based. Although presented in the context of America, the Nehemiah Postulates are highly relevant to all affluent nations and all pockets of affluent people in other nations around the World.

Section A: The Impending Decline of America (Postulates 1, 2, and 3)

1. A massive decline in the quality of life of Americans (and [people in] other affluent nations) is highly probable in the coming few decades, perhaps very soon. The disruptive causes are not likely to include extensive warfare within the affluent homelands, but rather a severe economic downturn prompted by one or more of the following circumstances:

A. Military & terrorist conflicts: One or more nuclear devices explode in major American or European cities, with long-term costly efforts toward retaliation, reconstruction and prevention.
B. Economic upheaval: Defaults by foreign debtors; credit-card debts and mortgage mismanagements; loss of economic confidence as experienced during the Great Depression.
C. Energy crisis: Peak oil becomes reality; major disruption in oil supply; fuel rationing.

D. Environmental disasters: Earthquakes, deforestation, soil erosion, water pollution, and increasing ravages from global warming, including droughts, hurricanes and rising sea level.

E. Continuation without changes: "Business-as-usual" piles up national and personal debt while resource depletion reduces options for action while facing increased international competition. Add here the insidious advances of drugs, crime, selfishness, and the decline of family values.

F. Combinations: Several of the above amplify each other in their downward spirals.

2. The diminished lifestyles of America's lower and middle classes would be unpleasant or at least significantly inferior to "the good life" of today. We should expect:

A. Housing: Limited winter heating; no air conditioning; foreclosures; shared housing.

B. Infrastructure: Minimal repair on roads, *etc.*; increasing breakdowns of services.

C. Employment: Increased unemployment and under-employment; decreased income.

D. Transportation: Higher costs of personal travel and of all transported goods.

E. Political/military: Political instabilities that give rise to additional warfare.

F. Health, education and welfare: Decline in well-being; less preventive medicine.

G. Government response: Limited funds for large crises; acceptance of inflation.

3. The decline cannot be avoided by any of the standard measures being implemented by the American government or proposed by politicians campaigning in the recent election. Even our tremendous technical capabilities cannot avoid the decline. The long-term overall advancement of the World can occur without America at the forefront of development and prosperity. The fundamental problems that must be confronted are found at the heart of American society. The current American variations of democracy and capitalism (Cap-20) are critically flawed and need serious adjustment, but not abandonment. Otherwise these flaws will continue to suppress and hinder our great nation while others reach or even surpass us.

Section B: Understanding Power in America (Postulates 4, 5, 6, 7, 8, and 9)

4. The five realms of power are out of balance in America and around the World. Each realm has several expressions, with one expression of each realm being dominant in America. Each expression has its own "currency." The imbalances have already partially crippled America and must be addressed to avoid the impending decline. In a single table, the realms and expressions and currencies are overly simplified, but you will get the idea. Details are presented in Papers Nos. 3 through 8.

Realms of Power	Expressions in America	Currencies in America	Additional Expressions and Their Currencies
Governance:	Democracy	Influence by & upon Voters	Dictatorship w/ Edicts; Theocracy
Economics:	Capitalism	Money & other capital	Socialism w/ Labor; Feudalism
Religion:	Faiths: Christian	Prayers & beliefs	Non-Christian prayers & beliefs
Justice:	Law	Enforcement	Anarchy w/ Brute force; Scriptures
Love:	Caring	Service (Helpfulness)	Selfishness w/ Self-service; Hate / Jealousy

There are many variations in every item listed above. Do not assume any black or white dichotomies. For example, capitalism in America today includes major components from socialist thought and practices. Likewise, there exists no pure socialism anywhere on Earth. And there can be many corrupting influences that distort democracy, [capitalism], faiths, laws, and caring.

5. Economics and Capitalism: Money is the currency of capitalism within the Realm of Power called economics. But in America the power of money has tainted all of the other realms of power. Democracy in America is so overwhelmingly influenced by money that it is almost a mockery. Money in America severely impacts the legal system, many aspects of service, and even the religious fiber of our country. Therefore, several of the proposed solutions are directly related to bringing the power of money under control. Capitalism is not attacked. But it should be modified in serious ways to become "Capitalism for the Twenty-first Century," abbreviated as "Capitalism-21" or simply "Cap-21."

6. Governance and Democracy: Democracy in America is based on voting (usually by a disgracefully small percentage of the adult population) for elected officials who then have further democratic functions to propose and vote on legislation, with the executive branch to implement those laws. Unfortunately, America's democracy today is literally controlled by repeatedly re-elected "serial incumbents" who are seriously influenced by money from both the left and the right. This situation is totally legal, not because it is correct or fair, but because the laws passed by prior and current serial incumbents have set the stage for this travesty of capitalist-controlled democracy.

7. Religion and Faith: Religion is the set of beliefs of a person or society concerning the existence (or non-existence) and characteristics of some force greater than human beings, commonly summarized by the word "god or God." In general, religion fosters ethical living and promotes some concept of being nice to other people. America was founded upon beliefs in ethical living and notions that people should be good to one another, including the teaching of such values to each generation. In this regard, the American concepts of "church and state" are united, not separated. On the other hand, faiths (which are practiced religions) start to go their own ways, preaching their particular flavor of beliefs. The various faiths represent power to their believers. To be the chosen people of the gods (or of the one true God) is the ultimate claim of power. Likewise, the ultra-liberal non-believers have a "god" of permissiveness wrapped in the rhetoric of "freedom," even freedom to be offensive to others. When a person or nation believes that "God is on my side," many deeds for good or evil are accepted and justified, especially when coupled with money and votes. Unfortunately, extremist-Americans try to project the Republicans as arch-conservative evangelicals and the

Democrats as ultra-liberal sectarians, both with their serial-incumbents as high priests. We should marginalize the extremes at both ends and concentrate on our shared core values, as found in the "reasonable person standard."

<><><><><><><><><><><><><><><><><><><><><><><><><><><><><><><><><><>

The Fifteen Nehemiah Postulates
are in 4 main categories:
A. The Impending Decline of America
B. Understanding Power in America
C. Wealth in America
D. Outreach to the World

<><><><><><><><><><><><><><><><><><><><><><><><><><><><><><><><><><>

8. Justice and Law: Justice is the concept that fairness should prevail. Justice is intended to be something desirable for people. In order to minimize conflicts over different perceptions of justice, officials in power create rules. Laws are formalized rules to govern a nation, state, city, formal organization, or club. There can be great laws, good laws, poor laws, and unjust laws. Just because some authorized body has made a law does not make it fair. Powerful people make laws, in part to maintain their view of what is to be allowed. Laws in America favor those individuals, groups and businesses that have the most money or influence to affect general elections or elected representatives. Perhaps the best thing about laws in America is that the people can take actions to change any of the laws, if done according to the laws about changing laws. And even the law-changing laws can be changed by a rare challenge to the Supreme Court or possible amendment to the Constitution by democratic vote.

9. Love and Caring: Perhaps the truest expression of love is the service that people are willing to do for the benefit of others. Service is wonderful for the personal and national psyche. Service builds character in men and women, young and old. There can never be too much service. Service can be a major part of the way for America to regain and maintain its position in World leadership, and thereby avert the impending crisis and decline. And yet, except for some minor efforts related to environmental protection, almost nothing in current American capitalism (Cap-20) favors love and service. Service is to be a key component in Capitalism-21. Do not expect capitalist corpora-tions to seriously embrace service until either a) the shareholders demand it (by their votes or their buy/sell decisions) or b) democratically-enacted laws require or reward service efforts, especially from those persons and companies that already have an abundance of money and assets. Service can do much to prevent the decline of America. Instead of the government providing those services, consider their execution by well-to-do people and corporations with assets, motivated by sticks (taxes) or carrots (meaning-ful recognition of service and allowed deductions). America should place service as a currency to balance the power of money. I present a few ideas in other Papers.

Section C: Wealth in America (Postulates 10, 11, and 12)

10. Normally we speak of the lower, middle, and upper classes in America, realizing that a full range of classes actually exist through strata and combinations of education, income, net worth, family of birth, *etc.* But consider for a moment two classes at the extremes: sub-lower and super-upper classes. Sub-lower is below the absolute minimum level of acceptable living: marginal food supply, miniscule health care, very poor schools, intolerable housing, unemployment, victimization by criminals, generally despicable living. This is American poverty. For such poverty to exist in our affluent America is shameful! Helping these people rise out of the sub-lower class does not require uncontrolled welfare and handouts, and certainly not wealth redistribution. Receiving benefits also means these individuals accept some responsibilities, even entering into appropriately increasing contractual agreements.

11. At the opposite end of the monetary spectrum, the super-upper class has wealth beyond imagination, more tangible wealth than the World has ever seen. Accumulation of wealth is the symbol of masterful capitalism. To become a billionaire is an interim goal of the thousands of "centa-millionaires." Even the "deca-millionaires" cannot spend their wealth except to try to make more money, try to influence legislation to make favorable rules for those who have capital, or spend it on absolute non-essentials. Many of the wealthy have life-styles characterized by self-indulgent extravagance and waste. With few exceptions, the super-wealthy who make donations actually give a very small percentage of their gross wealth and income to improving America, even including the taxes they pay.

12. The contrast between the previous two paragraphs tells us something about why America is facing impending decline. There will always be rich and poor people; capitalism does and should reward efforts, within reason. But allowing the existence of sub-lower conditions of one's own fellow countrymen is a serious indicator of a society rotting from the inside and weakened against outside forces that would bring down everyone, rich and poor alike. Capitalism and democracy are still the best for America and the World, but significant revisions are needed. Welfare handouts cannot fix those sub-lower class problems; the people on the lower financial rungs need to become involved in improving America. Coordinated national programs are needed simultaneously at each needy location. No actions should be overly fancy or expensive. Just get the basics to everyone. The ten Nehemiah Proposals in Paper No. 10 address the inherent unfairness and outline ways to build a better America and a better World, including the basics of Capitalism-21. Rest assured, the solutions will require more "backbone" than the World has ever seen. Perhaps that is why no great nation has ever escaped decline.

Section D: Outreach to the World (Postulates 13, 14, and 15)

13. Now apply everything from the above twelve paragraphs to the World. The five Realms of Power remain unchanged and the affluent nations of Europe and a few other places are strikingly similar to America. But elsewhere in the World's other great culture blocks, the expressions and currencies can be quite different. Some societies are unprepared for democracy; billions of people are at the edge or outside of any capital-based economy; non-Christian faiths have powerful followings; corrupt laws or virtual lawlessness ravage some nations; and service beyond one's family is questionable in many locations. On a World scale, the sub-lower true-poverty class also includes "sub-sub-sub-lower" people that, by American standards, are below the imaginable existence levels. Destitution or massive true poverty conditions for hundreds of millions of people include near starvation, zero health care, illiteracy, no clean drinking water, shacks or tents, unemployment, child labor, forced labor, criminals in total control, and even genocide. This is intolerable and absolutely shameful in a World where people of modest-to-super-affluent means live wastefully and selfishly and willfully ignorant of those in astonishing need. These factors extensively contribute to why great nations have declined and fallen. The dire poverty of others is a threat to America and affluent nations everywhere. Especially in the new "globalized" World, the problems of poverty abroad are rightfully our problems to solve.

◇◇

The affluent societies of the World have the resources to rectify the conditions of the sub-lower classes in nations that would cooperate.

◇◇

14. Without question, the affluent societies of the World have the resources to rectify the conditions of the sub-lower classes in nations that would cooperate. That is, IF the affluent nations would do that same task in their own nations and also reach out to the cooperating others. Those that do help should be appreciated, gain international friends, and avert many of the dangers of the impending decline. America should show its leadership abilities (or follow any other nations with the decency to do what is fair for disadvantaged people). America could enjoy a controlled economic recovery and boom with a vigorous "peace and development initiative." Proposals are provided in Nehemiah Paper No. 10, with details in later Papers.

15. America can avoid the impending decline by reviewing and revising its own democratic capitalism (that is, creating Capitalism-21) and simultaneously implementing a worldwide initiative for true-poverty elimination. Such a worthy cause will not be accomplished easily. Ironically, such efforts can help sustain and even grow the economies of the participating affluent nations. The economic advantages of waging war (with increased employment, factory production, R&D, *etc.*) can also be received by pursuing peace, minus the destructive aspects of warfare. Some of the necessary tasks will take years. Others can be accomplished by enacting a few laws. But we must begin now.

Commentary:

A "postulate" (noun) is a statement that someone (in this case, the I. M. Nehemiah author(s)) claims to be true and upon which further discussion is based. I have provided fifteen postulates that are interrelated. If any of the Nehemiah Postulates are proven to be false, then the others are also suspect and the *Nehemiah Papers* possibly could be ignored. I expect the very first postulate (about the impending decline of America) is the one that will be attacked most. That postulate refers to the future, and therefore it cannot be proven false until the future has actually occurred. I mention several times in the later Papers the year 2050, which is close enough to be reached in the life span of most Americans under the age of 40 in 2008. So, the issue really is whether you are willing to risk your own well-being and that of your children and grandchildren by denying the postulate that cannot be disproved for at least two decades, not discussing them, and not doing anything suggested in the Nehemiah Proposals and other Papers. Even if several of the Postulates are incorrect or only partially correct, I prefer to seek major actions for correcting the problems of America and the World. To simply wait or do minor actions for what could be quite devastating to America is not advisable.

I am counting on many Americans to take up the battle cry and to actually participate. Beware of false prophets and the status quo. Please read and discuss the next Papers. Demand action. Better yet, be active. Join me for *Building a Better America and a Better World*.

I hope that I have your attention. I am not a prophet of doom. Instead

I. M. Nehemiah
Setting the stage for a better World

The Nehemiah Proposals
[Paper No. 10 of the Nehemiah Papers]
I. M. Nehemiah © November 2008

The ten Nehemiah Proposals presented in this paper are based upon the fifteen Postulates presented in Paper No. 9. Please remember that the Nehemiah Postulates include:

America is heading for a life-changing decline;

The Five Realms of Power are out of balance in America;

American capitalism incorrectly dominates American democracy; and

The impending decline can be averted through democratic revisions of our laws, placing service as a currency to balance the power of money, and by implementing Capitalism-21.

Concerning Governance and Democracy:

Proposal #1: Strict term limits: A qualified American candidate should be eligible for only ONE term of office in one position, in succession. For example, after a two-year term, a U.S. Representative can immediately run for a seat in the U.S. Senate, or for other Federal, State, and local offices, but not for the House of Representatives until he or she has been replaced in that position for at least two years. New, incoming elected officials are usually quite competent people, so rest assured that effective representative governance would continue and actually thrive with more people involved. And the self-serving influence of PACs (Political Action Committees) and lobbyists will be better controlled and better exposed to the people. Career politicians (those who make a career out of being elected) are experienced in fund-raising and election campaigns having an incumbent's advantage. Stop them now.

Note 1: U.S. Presidents are currently allowed to have only two terms of office, without reference to being sequential or not. If the one-term limit is applied also to the Presidency, a qualified American candidate could be President for even three or more times, but not in sequence. Considering the consequences of the second terms of current and former Presidents George W. Bush, Bill Clinton, Ronald Reagan, and Richard Nixon, prohibition of sequential terms for Presidents seems like a rather good idea.

Note 2: In the political conventions of the Democratic party, the "superdelegates" are basically high-level politicians who represent the "establishment" and perhaps the worst (and the best, if there is any) of political machines in America. The vast majority of Americans do not have any influence on how the parties conduct their business, but we should be watchful and wary.

Concerning Economics and Capitalism:

Proposal #2: Attack, reduce, and virtually eliminate government waste and corruption: Earmarks and pork-barrel appropriations must be eliminated. Subsidies for favored groups must be rigorously reexamined with open disclosures to eliminate further favors for those already affluent. Close examination and monitoring could identify corruption that should be exposed and prosecuted. New laws and enforcement of existing laws must be put into practice.

Entitlements must be reevaluated, especially those going into the hands of the affluent. Someone previously favored by one or more former laws (enacted by lawmakers under the influence of various sources of money) is not entitled to benefits while other income and assets are substantial. Enough is enough. Entitlement payments can destroy the national economy while placing much money into the hands of those who hardly need it. Progressive reduction of such benefits also applies to those who have enough for a rather comfortable living. In all cases, entitlements must be reexamined and appropriated with care, with reinstatement of prior benefits when one's quality of life has declined to moderate levels.

One idea is that the entitlements currently going to affluent people could be stopped and saved in an account for later distribution IF the person or spouse ever drops to a lower middle-class lifestyle. This is similar to paying for an insurance policy against poverty during life, except it is not paid out upon the person's death. Note: If it is not legal to restrain entitlements based on financial situations, then alter the tax codes to re-claim that entitlement money back to the government that made the payments.

Let's begin at the top. This control of entitlements should apply first and foremost to the past Presidents and Vice Presidents who could collect their entitlements if and when their enormous incomes from speaking engagements, consultancies, donor support, *etc.* drop below a half-million dollars per year. The same should apply to all legislators. Entitlements should go to those whose well-being depends on that income, not to people who are feathering their affluent nests.

Likewise, wasteful spending toward ineffective social welfare programs must also be reexamined and stopped where appropriate, as discussed in Proposal #7.

◇◇

The ten proposals of Nehemiah relate to the Five Realms of Power:
A. Governance and Democracy (1)
B. Economics and Capitalism (2 & 3)
C. Religion and Faith (4 & 5)
D. Justice and Law (6 & 7)
E. Love and Caring (8, 9 & 10)

◇◇

Proposal #3: Modernize American economics with appropriate controls on massive wealth. In Capitalism for the 21st Century (Capitalism-21), very wealthy individuals, corporations, and organizations are encouraged to financially sponsor acceptable projects to assist sub-lower class people and neighborhoods to rise to levels where fairness for opportunity is more clearly evident. Recognition of the people and businesses that provide this financial assistance should be highlighted. In recompense, laws could allow massive deductions on income tax returns to offset what would otherwise be very high additional taxes on windfall profits, superstar incomes, and astronomical wealth never intended as a product of capitalism. The wealthy would essentially have the choice to have a say in where and how a significant portion of their vast income is spent, or to turn that money over to the U.S. Government (via tax legislation) for use in corresponding service efforts. One immediate objective could include the accomplishment of the United Nations' Millennium Development Goals. Always remember that the focus is to lift people from the sub-lower true poverty classes in America or overseas. In assisting the very needy, we must also solve serious problems as outlined in Proposals #6 and #7.

Concerning Religion and Faiths:

Preparatory note: America and the World are again faced with conditions in which the one true God has apparently selected two or more different societies as the chosen people at the same time. At least that is what fundamentalist Christians and fundamentalist Muslims would have us believe, although each would have us believe only their half of the condition. Other religions also have fervent believers. Even within religions there are serious differences that consume enormous amounts of time, efforts, resources, and sometimes blood. The resultant power struggles within and between the religious faiths contribute to the causes of the decline of nations.

Proposal # 4: Religious tolerance: If God is on your side, do not tell anyone; prove it silently by your humane actions. This cannot be made into a law in America. There is no harm in saying something like "God bless you" or "Allah be with you" to most other Americans. But overseas in some societies, zealot Christianity does not gain friends. Instead, this proposal is a statement to encourage Americans to do more and preach less. However, for learning and strengthening the core American values of ethical behavior and good deeds, the best locations to visit are generally the various places of worship (and not places of self-gratification). There is a strong connection between this Proposal #4 and Proposal #10.

Proposal # 5: As congregations and as individuals, do more for others through sharing and sacrifice. "Go the extra mile," and even further so that America earns respect and appreciation. Do more as religious congregations. Separation of church and state does not prohibit one-way non-religious assistance by churches to help the state to accomplish its non-religious objectives of government, such as having adequate school buildings or providing disaster relief (while implementing Proposal #4 above). Make sacrifices as individuals (see Proposals #7 and #8). Make sacrifices as a nation through wise selection of representatives to instruct the American government to make some sacrifices to benefit others. Always be sure that domestic and foreign assistance is what is appropriate and appreciated, not imposed militarily or for our own economic advantage. And do not waste assistance on corrupt people and programs that do not live and align according to the Nehemiah Postulates and Proposals.

Concerning Justice and Law:

Proposal # 6: Massive crack-down on drugs, organized crime, and social vices. Great nations fall from power because internal rot has weakened them, making them vulnerable to outside aggression or economic blackmail. Too much prosperity can lead to tolerance of forces that weaken the moral fiber of the society.

There must be no societal tolerance for recreational (non-medical) use of addictive drugs. The demand must be eliminated. The distribution system must be destroyed. Then the supply will wither and can be stopped.

Likewise, organized crime must be crushed by unyielding and stepped-up enforcement of current or additional laws. Punishments delivered by judges and juries should [always consider rehabilitation, but] be [appropriately] severe; forced hard labor in undesirable conditions with simple, health-sustaining food should be seen as a just penalty for all despicable criminal segments of society. Fear of such conditions of incarceration might become a deterrent for some potential criminals. Bad behavior in prison is punished with increased severity. Cooperate or eat only what is sufficient to sustain life.

Lesser social vices of drinking, smoking, and gambling would still be allowed but at heavy monetary prices proportionate to the vice's destructive effect on health and social welfare. Partakers must comply with watchdog efforts to nip any excesses at the very first signs. One example is the immediate immobilization of any vehicle (using boots or chains or breathalyzers in cars) operated by a person who leaves a bar with an alcohol level above the legal limit. Another is the financial review of frequent gamblers and their family conditions, with required counseling if problems initiate.

Proposal # 7: Family-style "tough love" to be applied to society and welfare programs. To be nice, gentle, and sympathetic to a person in trouble is admirable [and be part of rehabilitation], but too much tolerance can be easily abused. As it is in the family, so it is also in society. The welfare system must be overhauled and enhanced with far greater vigilance while being understanding. America's welfare system is under-funded for the supervision needed to stop the over-payment of benefits. An American form of "contractual welfare" should be developed. The minimum wage rate does not need to rise IF corresponding financial benefits (such as part of health care costs) to both employees and employers are arranged through related legislation. Our society must open the doors to semi-employment of people who have mental or physical difficulties coping with regular life in America. With extremely few exceptions, Americans on welfare between 16 and 70 years of age are able to do something in exchange for social services and monetary support. Physically challenged persons could be great tutors or story readers or assistants in a local school if transportation is made available, thereby working and contributing to justify their monthly support payment. As a guideline, many welfare recipients should be involved in some approved activity for at least the number of hours at minimum wage that would relate to the amount of their welfare check and services. Some of those activities could be job training. This should involve more financial support (not just from taxes, but also from charities) and supervisory labor (see Proposal #9 below) than in the current system while reducing the net amount paid to recipients.

Concerning Love and Caring:

Proposal # 8: Compulsory national service for every man and woman, young and old. This is universal compulsory service. If you live in America or claim American citizenship, you must serve, and not just once.

For adults under the age of thirty, there are two parts: A. Basic military training of four to eight months, and B. A cumulative period of at least two years of service prior to age thirty either 1) in the military (which will have redefined tasks to include building up friendly nations as well as destroying enemies), or 2) in a massively expanded existing or new service program (*e.g.,* Peace Corps and AmeriCorps), or 3) in approved private or non-governmental programs of meaningful service (excluding promotion of specific faiths) defined according to skills needed for building a better America and World.

For those aged thirty to sixty, an additional cumulative thirty months of service (average of one month per year) to be defined by laws, or perhaps a well-paid person could make a payment of money equal to thirty months of gross income at the person's highest earning level.

For those over the age of sixty, appropriate programs to give service would be made available for capable seniors and retirees from a coalition of public and private agencies plus individual initiatives. The "Gray Corps" [or "Senior Corps"] could accomplish much, especially in America, but also overseas for those who are willing and able.

Reasonable but low wages and core benefits would be provided in relation to the duties of service. Abundant recognition should be given for service rendered.

Proposal # 9: Make "service" an alternative to money as a capitalist "currency" with corresponding power. In addition to service measured as time and effort, there is also service provided by financial resources. People who are very good at making money are to be recognized and rewarded in non-material ways for their provision of money to do the necessary functions of government and society. This is part of the revised economic system called Capitalism-21 (see Proposal #3 above). For example, "Corporation X" might have a Super Bowl advertisement about its service efforts and include its logo formed by people in colored T-shirts who live in the area being served. Some of the large service projects could improve some of the worst conditions in America's worst neighborhoods, or tackle environmental protection efforts such as reforestation for a devastated area, or build, equip, and staff educational improvement in a selection of impoverished high schools internationally. Individuals can perform direct services (as in Proposal #8) or as stock shareholders who vote to instruct publicly traded corporations to undertake humanitarian actions, invest in environmental protection, and place limits on executive salaries.

Proposal #10: Bring order and decency into American society. For some people there is a fine line between correct and incorrect behavior; for others there is a wide gray area between good and bad. And the line or gray area can shift left (liberal or permissive) and right (conservative or intolerant) depending on who or what is involved. Throughout history, when prosperity arrives, permissiveness increases and eventually the whole society confronts decline. Sometimes a society or sub-group can save itself for a while with some self-imposed strictness; more often the decline is very serious or even devastating. Civil liberties are good, but they can be taken so far as to critically weaken even the greatest of nations. When rational limits are being abandoned, society can suffer the "tyranny of freedom." One example: parental rights should not include the liberty to injure children physically, educationally, emotionally, or in any way which harms the child's future. A parent on drugs (including alcoholism) should lose rights and face active surveillance, [rehabilitation], even household monitoring. America must come to grips with its internal decay and impose and enforce reasonable laws. This decay is a major reason for unsafe neighborhoods, substandard learning in schools, excessive need for social services, and much of the cause for unemployment. The same rules also apply to the rich, famous, and powerful who even flaunt their use of drugs and their exemption from full prosecution. A democracy must be able to control its own worst factions. Freedom is not free, and liberty is not absolute. Until America confronts the need for limits on liberty [/license], the nation will further polarize and will fail to be one nation.

Commentary:

You could be thinking that these proposals are idealistic and impossible. Think again.

Proposals #1 (term limits) and #4 (religious tolerance) cost virtually nothing to implement if the population of America decides to adopt them. And the benefits would be substantial.

Proposal #2 (eliminate waste) should save far more government money than it costs to implement and supervise. All the elected officials talk about this. Now is the time to actually accomplish this task.

Proposal #6 (stop drugs and crime) is common sense about immediate and continual help for our fellow Americans. Although it will require significant funding at the start, eventually there will be lower costs, then recovery of the investment, and finally financial dividends to the whole society.

Proposal #7 (tough-love for welfare) might save money in the long run, but actually more money is needed initially for firm and fair implementation of targeted efforts to have every American as gainfully employed as possible.

Proposals #3, #5, #8, #9 and #10 (each with individual commentary below) are related as parts of Capitalism-21 economics to help America possibly avoid the impending decline. They are expensive. They are not popular. They are not easy to accomplish. But they are fair. And they will show to the World that America is fair and caring and interested in more than the almighty dollar.

Proposal #3 (tapping the power of massive wealth) is a large part of obtaining sufficient financial resources to accomplish fair Capitalism-21 objectives to eliminate extreme poverty and [reduce] social problems. The important difference proposed is the option for [payor-] directed funding instead of turning money over to the government via taxes. Use wealth to provide service (as in Proposal #9).

Proposal #5 (sacrifice for others) is a war cry, a call for helping others. But it has no legislative teeth, no programs, and no evident expenses. But if accepted by the American people, it can move mountains for accomplishing Proposals #8 and #9 and perhaps others yet to appear.

Proposal #8 (compulsory national service) will be expensive to implement, but the national gains are numerous:

A. Increased employment. National service might be paid as low, non-taxable income, but it will put millions of Americans to work in important jobs and keep them able to make purchases that help make our economy strong.

B. Strengthened national security: Every able-bodied young man and women will have military basic training. Some will enlist in the "armed services" and be better paid when on duty in conflict areas. Many others will discover that regular (peace-time) military service will provide additional career training and travel opportunities, especially on "peace services" related to road and building construction, education, communications, medical corps, and advanced technologies.

C. Improved American presence abroad: The much-expanded Peace Corps will train and employ teachers, community development leaders, and medical staff to go into cooperating impoverished societies, but with stronger goals and more resources for sustainable local impact than is currently possible. Coupled with similar service-people from the other affluent nations, there could be literally millions of educated and motivated caring people who seek to bring the sub-lower-class people up to at least minimal decency in day-to-day living.

D. Qualified people for homeland improvement: At whatever age, the participants in national service will be available to correct the sub-lower-class problems inside of America. This will include compulsory time by some of America's greatest minds and stars and business executives who will help create jobs and solve problems. To serve honorably in America's national services should become a highlight in everyone's eyes.

◇◇◇

The Nehemiah Proposals are an attempt to bring capitalism under control in a way that strengthens America for the benefit of rich and poor alike.

◇◇◇

Proposal #9 (service as an alternative to money) is a cornerstone of the proposals. It says that people who have abundant money and assets are asked to diminish their rate of capital accumulation and even significantly reduce their assets until such time that the sub-lower-class has been elevated to at least minimal levels worldwide. This is a key part of Capitalism-21. Voluntary participation in this alternative is highly unlikely. Compulsory participation comes in two types: A) taxes that designate the U.S. Government as the agent responsible for spending the funds for the needed efforts, or B) contributions appropriately acknowledged on tax forms for acceptable activities chosen by the contributor, even with his or her personal direction regarding the application of the funds. Use the stick to prod, or the carrot to entice, or some of both if needed.

Proposal #10 (order and decency) will be argued for years and fought in countless courtrooms. I have intentionally not been specific. If America is unwilling to tackle the issues of the other nine proposals, number ten will be of little consequence. Order and decency will not occur if America cannot implement plans for the control of money over our democracy, term limits, ending government waste, stopping crime, appropriate welfare, restrictions on runaway wealth, national service by everyone, and massive international assistance. But if America can bring itself to address the first nine proposals, then the natural collateral outcomes will include the insistence that American children attend schools where teachers are respected, the police [and local assistants] are empowered to enforce laws in all neighborhoods, and freedom of speech and the right to bear arms are protected but not exaggerated beyond the norms of rational civilized society.

None of this will be easy to accomplish. But it will be worth every bit of effort!

* * * * * * * *

Finally, just in case you missed something, here are four eye openers.

First, this is not an attempt to destroy capitalism; it is an attempt to bring capitalism under control in a way that strengthens America for the benefit of rich and poor alike. Throughout America's history, those with wealth have always been advantaged by the game rules of capitalism. Controls have been implemented (and some removed) during past centuries, but now is the time for a significant additional revision that is tentatively called "Capitalism-21."

Second, our scope is the entire World. America can never live alone in this modern globalized World. We must have as many friends as possible.

We cannot buy them. We must earn their friendship. Then they will assist us in the quest for stability that can avert the impending decline of America and other places. With the implementation of the ten Proposals, we will set a good example. Of course we should expect other affluent nations to do similar good things (and many of them are already ahead of us on some of these issues). And affluent individuals in the developing nations should also participate.

Third, we must be firm with those who are unfair to us or to their own people. I am thinking of the affluent individuals in the developing countries who have historically been unfair to their own people. Some will change, some others we can ignore, and some others we can pressure, but never should we allow our assistance to be misused by corrupt persons in needy societies. America is to regain its position of being a true champion for justice. Capitalism-21 is NOT a blind give-away program. Recipients of assistance are not required to give up their rights of independence or cultural heritages, but universal aspects of decency and order and fairness must be incorporated and clearly evident in every culture assisted. Later essays will deal with some actual and probable situations. Expect surprises.

Fourth, when viewed on a worldwide basis, over seventy percent of Americans are in the "very affluent" category. Therefore, almost everyone should expect to pay something for the accomplishment of the ten Nehemiah Proposals. After all, we Americans (and people in other affluent situations) have been living quite well for decades while other human beings cope with starvation, illiteracy, poor health, *etc*. Our expenditures and efforts will be a small price compared to having a massive decline in American living.

Please remember that I am one of you.

I. M. Nehemiah
Your neighbor

Equality, Justice and Economic Levels in American Capitalist Democracy
[Paper No. 11 of the Nehemiah Papers]
I. M. Nehemiah © March 2008

Equality and justice are not the same. Justice is fairness, while equality is equal-ness. To be fair does not mean the same thing as to be equal. But to be highly unequal in certain circumstances can be grossly unfair. In other words, we need to better understand equality and justice. And yes, this does relate very much to the issues to prevent the impending decline of America.

All people are equal under God, can cast one vote in a democracy, and have unalienable rights to life, liberty, and the pursuit of happiness. I needed to say that. I believe that. But that does not mean equal pay or equal prestige or even equal achievement of happiness.

The concept of equality has two serious problems that are closely related:

1.   The first problem with "equality" is that people only desire it with those who have more than they do.
2.   The second problem with "equality" is that people only desire that people with less than they do should rise up to their level.

People advocate bringing other people up to their level, or for themselves to rise to superior levels. Nobody is willing to move downward to the lower levels.

People are not equal. The most obvious examples are when individual persons are measured and then compared. These unequal attributes include intelligence, physical abilities, and socio-psychological skills. Slow learners with physical challenges and poor social graces do not become corporate executives, movie stars, great athletes, or eloquent speakers/politicians. The deck is stacked against some people early on and throughout their lives, while others have so many favorable personal attributes to help them succeed, even to become rich and famous.

People are not equal. Inherited wealth, powerful friends, and being in the right place at the right time give some people the upper hand either by birth or through gradual acquisition in life by hard work or luck or even cheating. The stories of the origins (and declines) of the wealth of a person or family are often colorful, even told in books, films and songs. The American stories reveal much about American capitalism and society, not all of which is very nice. For example, some families have extreme wealth that originated a few generations back with the then legal but now frowned upon dastardly deeds of monopolies, insider trading, unfair practices, and even dealing with drugs and slave traffic. Such was capitalism then, and the fortunes remain intact in the "old-money" families while the descendents of the then-disadvantaged have no recourse for adjustment.

People are not equal. But they all deserve justice and fairness.

Fairness

What is fair? Fairness is mainly decided by the society in consultation with religion and laws and human compassion/caring. But society can be viciously "unfair" at times, even at opposite extremes. Consider the now-discredited experiments with communistic socialism that brutally stripped all assets from the wealthy and middle classes, only to reestablish inequality based on ideological power and influence. Consider also the outwardly capitalist democracies in developing countries that have created inhumane conditions for masses of people living in dire poverty while relatively few others have extreme wealth, at times even defended by America. The grossly lopsided Capitalism-18 in dictator Somoza's

Nicaragua was held in higher regard than the socialistic readjustments in (weakly democratic) Sandinista Nicaragua, even leading to illegal dealings of Reagan's Iran-Contra scandal.

Likewise, some sharp executives who make great salaries and even bonuses create their new fortunes while their companies are actually progressively failing. They might resign or be fired when the stocks go south, but they keep their fortunes. In the infamous Enron bankruptcy (and other less colorful cases), many executives retained millions of dollars while shareholders (including investment banks and pension funds) took extensive losses to their portfolios. Even worse, many Enron employees lost their jobs and most of the value of their retirement plans. Capitalism-20 as practiced today in America is not so great and wonderful as the wealthy people would like us to believe.

◇◇◇

People are not equal. But they all deserve justice and fairness.

◇◇◇

Just consider pyramid selling that enriched the first few and left the latecomers with dubious inventories, until laws made it an illegal practice. And consider marketing and selling techniques that promote unnecessary purchases, even to (or especially to) the vulnerable less-educated or elderly segments of society. The credit card companies want you to be in debt so that they can apply very high interest to the overdue balance. These are examples of businesses earning large amounts of money by legally taking advantage of others while claiming to provide needed services. For some, maybe the services are useful. For many, certainly not.

Another interesting aspect of American capitalism is that the capitalist players (investors, corporations, land owners, etc.) want to keep the full profits and growth of the investment when times are good, including windfall profits and government subsidies. But when things go bad they call for the government to bail them out of trouble. Examples:

1) Many pension funds have been under-funded or "depleted" (robbed?) by corporations and even state governments, with the US government providing guarantees via the Pension Benefit Guaranty Corporation (PBGC). In the United Airlines pension bailout in 2004, the PBGC took charge of $6.6 billion of the $9.8 billion of unfunded accrued benefits. 2) Profitable

home building and businesses are located on known floodplains, with emergency relief funds provided occasionally. 3) Government subsidies are paid for farm production, with some years having great profits that the farmers get to keep, but in years when drought or blight or other hardship occurs, the assistance is massive. All this is done under the name of Capitalism. To speak against it is not to favor Socialism, but to seek significant changes in Capitalism-20 that is failing our nation.

I am not against the government programs; they are important to assure some stability in the naturally troubled world. But the corporations and property owners and farmers should not be allowed to rake in the business profits and increases in property values without corresponding payment of taxes or profit sharing or some other mechanism to cover for those stability benefits. We like the security provided by our government, but we allow people and corporations to become very rich in the good times (and not pay big taxes or profit sharing) and then avoid the financial consequences when the bad times come, even if caused by poor management by the highly paid executives. Capitalism in America needs some fixing both at the top end where the assets are, and also at the bottom end where serious unfairness needs to be rectified.

People are not equal. But they all deserve justice and fairness.

What is fair? As I have said, fairness is mainly decided by the society (our democracy) in consultation with religion and laws and human compassion/caring (three of the Realms of Power). Tradition can be important, but tradition represents the past, and we know that the past is often different from the present. America needs to adjust its policies about the very wealthy and the very poor. The old models of capitalism are not "gospel" that cannot be changed. Fortunately, America is not beyond hope. But we must open our eyes. There is unfairness in America, as discussed below. I. M. Nehemiah does not name individuals as examples, but we can look at examples like Enron and also at the data of our whole society.

Social Classes and Income Levels in America

Let's consider some census-derived income numbers, generic names for status and classes, and estimates of assets. There are exceptions higher and lower in every classification.

Table of Social Classes and Income Levels in America

Social Status	Economic Class	Income Category	Dollar Income (household) (in 2008)	Assets (not income) (est. 10% growth/yr)	% of Pop.
Highest Third of American Households					
Elite	Super-upper	Ultra-rich	>$500K to millions	$20 million to billions	< 1%
(Some of the Elite have modest income while having massive assets, and vice versa)					
Exec/Prof	High-upper	Very rich	$250K - $500K	$2 - $20 million	~ 1%
(Note: Top 20% of population has over $90K household income, which equals 50% of total USA income.)					
(Educated guess: Top 20% of population owns over 85% of America's net worth; top 5% might have 50%.)					
Prof/Business	Low-upper (or Super-middle?)	Basic-rich	$70K - $250K	$100K - $2 million	~30%
Middle Third of American Households					
White Collar	High-middle	Well-to-do	$50K - $70K	Home plus investments	~15%
Mixed	Low-middle	Comfortable	$30K - $50K	~$50K Home equity	~18%
Lowest Third of American Households					
Blue Collar	High-lower (or Sub-middle?)	Struggling	<$30K	~$10K - Vehicle, furniture	~13%
Poverty	Low-lower	Into poverty	<$20K	About zero	~10%
(Note: An individual earning less than $10K per year, and a household of 4 earning less than $20K are officially in poverty in America. They equal about 20% of US population.)					
Welfare	Sub-lower	Marginalized (incl. Welfare)	<$10K	Less than debts	~10%

Consider the people in the "sub-lower-class" who are truly disadvantaged with very low below-poverty incomes, poor education, no health services, *etc*. It is proper and decent to want them to rise higher, with appropriate assistance such as "contractual welfare." Note that I did not say "to be raised higher" via unrestricted handouts. These sub-lower-class people are primarily recipients of welfare, but the benefits are rather meager and not resolving the problems. In addition, many of the people in the lowest third on the socio-economic ladder are also "slow learners" in the lowest third of mental ability. Granted that many of them have successful lives. Forrest Gump is an exaggerated example, but he helps us understand these people. But then add in "poor attitudes," as found in grumpy and disagreeable people. It is extremely difficult to assist them because their "rights" allow them to be nasty even to the social workers and their own families (parents and adult children) who want desperately to assist but are blocked from even interacting with the welfare agencies to assist their "loved ones in need." This must be addressed.

A notch higher, people in the "low-lower-class" are in poverty or on the edge. They generally have some low-paid employment, receive some benefits, have weak or no health insurance, live in poor neighborhoods with excessive violence, and attend poor schools. Their contributions to and eventual benefits from Social Security are low. Their taxable-income bracket is about zero percent. They are burdened with debts at high interest rates. Many do not manage well their meager income and assets.

Example: If one single person earns $7.50 per hour, that is $15K annual gross wages and he or she is not in poverty. But if that same person is in a household of four and supports a spouse and two children (or one child and dependent parent), they are officially in poverty. A second job, or working spouse, can elevate them, but money is scarce for even some basic expenses. No savings. They face potential disaster if struck by job-loss, another pregnancy or illness. Their housing and neighborhood and schools are likely to be marginal.

Please note that I am not advocating handouts without requiring some responsibility. People who receive the assistance should behave "appropriately" with actions such as seeking employment and further education, including compulsory money-management instruction and monitoring. An American variation of "contractual welfare" would be appropriate. I am advocating serious efforts to overcome the causes of the poverty and raise these people into the upper ranks of the lower class, from which they and their children will have reasonable lives and realistic opportunities for upward mobility if desired.

The moderate-income earners (those having $[40]K to $70K gross household incomes for the middle third of American households) are doing okay, [subject to regional variations of the cost of living]. They want more, but actually they could share some of their well-being and still live comfortably even in a smaller home, with an older car, and taking a more modest vacation. This "sharing" is already partially implemented in American life through taxation systems and voluntary donations to worthy causes. They complain about taxes, but they are willing to pay for needed schools and services in their communities. More taxes on them do not seem appropriate unless there is some nationally defined need. This core of the middle class in America has "enough" for their pleasant lives, but many of them create their own problems because they save too little, many spend too much on unnecessary items, struggle with credit card debt, are too self-indulgent, and do not see much (if any) increase in their net worth. Sure they would like to have more income and assets, but they also want security now and in the future. They will not move to the poor side of town. The national debt and personal debt are major threats to their well-being. The Nehemiah Postulates about impending decline for America really concern them. Or should, because a decline will have the greatest negative impacts on their lives and on their children's lives. They are vulnerable in part because they have been lulled by the prosperity of the past twenty-five years.

The basic-rich people are "doing quite well" and have household incomes of $70K to $250K per year. Some are starting their careers; others are ready for retirement soon. So much variation can lead to quibbling about definitions that is not appropriate for this discussion now. Just note that these people can purchase anything except the highest luxury items. If they want a boat, they can buy it. The same for extremely lovely homes, lavish vacations, private schools, fancy cars, or whatever else is highest on their priorities. But they cannot do all of those things at the same time. Many simply invest more and more. They appreciate ownership not just of their homes, but also of assets that have the best rates of return. They are benefiting from the current American style Capitalism-20. Many have attained millionaire status or could in their lifetimes.

In reference to Capitalism-21

When discussing the very high-income people from $250K to millions of dollars per year, there are factors in addition to basic wages. One could be called "windfall wages." How much is the value of an hour of a person's efforts? If a person receives one million dollars for a year of employment, that is $500 per hour or $4000 per day. There are executives and television personalities and sport stars receiving $10 million per year, or $5000 per hour for forty hours per week. Note that they do pay many dollars in taxes, but certainly not over 35% taxes, after extensive deductions. They have major increases in their net worth every year. Perhaps they are worth that much. (Or perhaps not.) The point here is that these super-rich people do exist, and they continue accumulating money year after year after year while also living extremely lavish lives. For some, the **increase** (only the increase) in their net worth from salaries in one year is more than the **total** income of many Americans in an entire lifetime. That is American Capitalism-20 today. I will not feel sorry for the very wealthy people regardless of how high the taxes could go. They have learned to play the capitalist system well and to utilize their existing wealth to gain more and more. It is in their best interest to prevent changes in the current system. In my opinion, the current system must be changed if the nation is to become better off, and not just favor the wealthy people.

The second factor about very wealthy people relates to accumulated assets that provide additional income or asset growth. Assume that a wealthy person has $10 million in investment assets, excluding their million-dollar house and luxury personal items. Even at only 5% growth, that places $500,000 of increased net worth onto his or her financial statement every year. Many receive much more than 5%, and many have far more than $10 million. There are numerous people with $100 million or more in assets, called "centi-millionaires," who are still far from the billionaire category or the "deca-billionaire" level. Because America's tax structures are enacted by "serial incumbent" legislators subjected to great influence by money, the rich people pay relatively low tax rates while their net worth climbs higher and higher. The gap between the rich and the poor in America is widening.

I do not say that the very wealthy people are bad or mean or crooked. Most of them are living according to the laws of traditional capitalist America. But I do say that when in America some children have substandard education and some elderly lack basic health care and some neighborhoods lack adequate police protection, a new look at fairness is required. It is only a matter of changing the laws and making sure that the new laws are "fair" even for the very rich. And in terms of impact on their existing lavish life-styles, there would be virtually zero impact. Even if the after-taxes increase in net worth was cut in half for a very wealthy person, they would have no need to make any changes in their life-styles.

Does that sound harsh? Think again. Imagine a very high income person. Let's exclude in this discussion any increase (capital gains) in the value of the person's assets like stocks, bonds and property. This very-high-income person pays taxes at current rates and still has an **increase in net worth** (including purchases of additional stocks, properties, etc.) of one million dollars in one year because of work or employment or consultancies, etc. My suggestion is that at least half of the million dollars should be applied to the improvement of the national well-being. We will be discussing later what could be considered as "improvement of the national well-being," but two clear examples are the improvement of substandard education and better enforcement of the laws in difficult neighborhoods. The high-income person would not suffer even the least of discomfort and would have greatly assisted the building of a better America. And if higher taxes cause them to lose the capitalist motivation to work hard, that is also okay because there are thousands of other very capable people earning far less now who would gladly take over those "unfulfilling" duties that some unpatriotic rich-guy or rich-girl does not want to do for a mere $500,000 salary.

◇◇

If substantially higher taxes cause highly paid people to lose the capitalist motivation to work hard, someone among the thousands of other very capable people will gladly take over those "unfulfilling" duties.

◇◇

["Sharing" by voluntary contributions or by much higher taxes on high income and high net worth] is an important part of Capitalism-21. Could this be done? Certainly. Here are four ways:

A. Good: Just change the laws in America. A willing Congress and an understanding President could do that in five months. Enacted by June 2009.
B. Better: Even without any changes in laws, the stockholders of major corporations could change their internal rules about salaries and start putting some serious money into building a better America and a better World.
C. Best: The high-income people could decide that they can do very well without so much increase in net worth and consequently make massive donations into projects that they (or people they hire) decide would be the approved initial pilots of what can be done to rectify the problems in America or overseas.
D. Better than best: All of the above in coordinated efforts.

Note to the rich folks: Do not worry too much. I do propose that rewards other than money should be forthcoming to offset the reduction of your grossly gross incomes. I do not ask you to like me. I just ask you to help change the course of American capitalism so that our great nation can continue on and on and on. America made you great. Now it is time for your grateful response.

Here are some quick items to note:

1. Although I am proposing the "half-of-net-worth-increase" money be applied to building a better America and a better World, I did not say that the money must be taken as a tax. In the spirit of free enterprise, the very high-income persons are encouraged to select one or more targets of improvement from a nationally prepared list of targets, and even to become personally involved with the target project of choice. If they decline, then an obligatory "assessment" should be made into law and implemented.

2. You think that still sounds harsh? Well, try living your life with a substandard education or in an unsafe neighborhood. THAT is harsh.

3. The objective is better equality up to but not much beyond the minimum standards of decency. Nehemiah Paper No. 13 discusses minimum standards.

4. Please remember that the writings of I. M. Nehemiah are about an impending decline of America. And the very wealthy people would also suffer with such a decline. We need to change some of the fundamentals of our society. What is described above is merely a changing of some of the rules or laws of capitalism. It is a shift to Capitalism-21. Yes, America would very much still be a capitalist nation, but with more compassion in appropriate, sustained, and constructive ways.

5. This is akin to authorizing massive donations (to approved non-religion-based projects for the national well-being) that could be taken into account with the yearly income tax filings.

6. This is not a free ride for the impoverished people. Standards will be set and imposed, as discussed in Nehemiah Paper No. 15 and elsewhere.

7. Consider also that the above model is to be applied to the average high-income earners who could increase their net worth by $50,000 in a year. They should contribute 50%, or maybe only 30%, even after living the great lives that they currently enjoy.

8. In our discussion we need to examine equality and the ways to make conditions fair for all. But even more than that, we need to find fair and equitable ways that also avoid or prevent the impending decline of America. And also not destroy or undermine what is good in capitalism in America.

9. Expect resistance. But respond in terms of justice and the need for fairness in capitalist American society. Our future depends upon our success.

I am not sure if I am happy or sad to have ruffled the feathers of some readers. I hope that you will think and talk about what I have written. All I know is that

> *I. M. Nehemiah*
> Conscience for fairness

Sources of Wealth in America
[Paper No. 12 of the Nehemiah Papers]
I. M. Nehemiah © March 2008

Six Ways to Get Rich

People obtain money and other assets in a variety of ways. Nations can become affluent in similar ways. Please consider this list:

1. **Hours of honest labor.** Some people do physical work; others have mental tasks (accountants, teachers, etc). They receive wages or salary somewhat related to skill levels. Not a fast way to get rich, but this can be sufficient for good living and can accumulate modest wealth over time. In fact, in a reasonable society, honest labor should be sufficient [income], assuming the availability of employment. For a nation, a skilled labor force is one key to prosperity.

2. **Money generates more money.** To have money or assets (perhaps by inheritance or even access to loans) gives opportunities to earn monetary interest or capital gains as in the stock market. Borrowed money (OPM = Other People's Money) that is well applied (as in a home mortgage or business ownership) can also bring gains in an expanding economy. Management of the money is required but can be hired. There are risks of losing the assets, but in general, money makes money. A nation that is wealthy has financial resources to become even wealthier.

3. **Physical resources.** Oil on Jed's land sent the Clampett family to Beverly Hills. Finding new resources can make a person wealthy.

Gold rushes, fertile cropland, abundant water, etc. contribute greatly to the wealth of a nation.

4. **Innovation and talent.** Creativity and unique abilities can bring great wealth. Invent something that can be marketed; create something special such as a song or computer program. Or perform is exceptional ways, as do outstanding talents like Tiger Woods, Elton John, Jackie Chan, Angelina Jolie and Stephan King. Originality can reap great rewards. For nations this could include progression to the Iron Age and Space Age and Information Age, plus the Agricultural Revolution.

5. **Good luck (including divine intervention).** Win the lottery, or inherit a fortune, have an extremely rich friend. For a nation, the hand of God striking down the opposition can be a great boost to prosperity.

6. **Take advantage of others.** Through legal tricks or real cheating or brute force, take wealth from others. Some people are very good at this, and so are some nations.

There are many combinations of the above that have led to great fortunes. Maybe I left out something, but this is a good start.

American Experiences with Race, Origins and Socio-economic Status

For individuals, any one of these six ways to wealth could be the major source of great affluence. To have two or more combining for success is even better. For America, all six have been important for reaching its current high level of prosperity. America has abundant natural resources and a tremendous labor force that produces well and also innovates in so many ways. Its wealth has accumulated over centuries without major warfare on its home soil (except the Civil War). Whether by good luck or divine intervention, America has been extremely fortunate. Of course, in the early years all of these lands were taken from the Native Americans, often by the Paleface-written laws or brute force and even massacres. But we can forget about that part because the tribal Indians were not using the lands as well as capitalist settlers could do.

"Whoa, wait a minute," say Tonto and Morning Flower! And I agree. I was just baiting the readers to see if you were awake. Pointing out that much of America's land was taken from the Native Americans emphasizes that poverty today among Native Americans cannot be justified while the settlers live in splendor. I am not going to debate that episode of American justice here. I am not arguing for compensation in Twenty-first century terms. The ancestors of Native Americas also migrated in and just took over the place. ("Finders keepers" does not give legal rights.) But I do say that major efforts to help any sub-lower-class Native Americans to rise up to minimum levels of decent living (education, health, [employment], etc) should be assisted by our nation, that is, by all residents here who have decent living conditions.

Also, I want to discuss how some of the national and personal bastions of accumulated wealth derived their advantage at the expense of others, mostly under the cover of traditional American-style legal Capitalism-18-19-20.

America was and still is a land of opportunity for immigrants. Over the centuries the new arrivals have attained good lives that for the very vast majority have been better here than in their countries of origin. By being in America these people have escaped many European wars that hurt those who did not migrate. Many Irish, Swedes, Italians, British, and other Europeans arrived in the 1800s to 1920s as penniless immigrants and most eventually found happiness here. They built railroads, other industries, and family farms in the heydays of American Capitalism-18-19 that launched our strong middle class. Wonderful. But check out the extremes. The barons of big business created massive fortunes, often by dubious means that were legal then. The Trust Busters introduced laws to limit the robber-baron monopolistic capitalism. Meanwhile others faced hardships as exploited low-wage laborers. But that is the "luck of the game" of traditional American capitalism, and if the ancestors of today's low-income white folks did not get on the gravy train back then, that's just too bad for them and their offspring.

"Whoa, wait a minute," say Sven and Ian and Sophia, and so do I. Just because some people have not prospered under American capitalism does not make them unworthy of receiving the basic fairness that this prosperous nation can provide. I did not say prosperity needed to be made equal. But fair at least for the basics. After all, the ancestors of white well-to-do

Americans got off the same boats as did ancestors of those who live in sub-lower conditions today.

Now consider the Afro-Americans. Although most of their ancestors came here as slaves, many have prospered. And some have attained truly great influence and wealth under capitalist principles of more prosperity for the "better" ones, that is the ones who work harder, are more intelligent, are more talented, are better connected, have better luck, and who can play the edges of legal games without getting caught. Even those in Afro-American ghettos today have far better lives than in the harsh fields and slums of poorly governed impoverished African nations. America's Blacks should be glad they are here and not in the jungles.

"Whoa," say Tom and Wilma and Bill, and so do I. Yes, the Afro-Americans are better off here, but that does not justify substandard education and lack of neighborhood security for America's Blacks. We can hope that the wealthy leadership (both Black and White) will massively support the Nehemiah Proposals that would allow them to significantly impact the fundamental issues of poverty. This is crucial to the success of Capitalism-21.

◇◇◇

The leadership of all segments of society should massively support the Nehemiah Proposals that significantly impact the fundamental issues of poverty.

◇◇◇

America's two current waves of immigrants come here mainly for financial benefits. One wave consists of skilled people because we select them for computer jobs, medical work and other professional-level employment. Our national policies favor this "brain drain" from developing countries into America. Bringing in skilled migrants is generally less expensive than paying for education and training of born-here Americans, so that helps keep the overall costs of such services from skyrocketing, and that improves business profits. The second wave has mainly Latinos / Hispanics with fewer skills except a willingness to do manual labor that most born-here Americans decline to do for minimum wages or even less. Again, in true capitalist style, businesses receive the financial advantages [of cheap labor], and prices are lower for Americans eating in restaurants or enjoying hand-picked fruits and vegetables or buying products from dubious businesses. Some Latinos are here illegally and leech off of our tax-supported schools, etc. They are lucky we do not try very hard to kick them out!!

"Pare, espera un momento," say Juan and Maria. But should anyone even listen to them? They are not even speaking English!! I say, yes, we must listen. And we must act. Something is wrong with current American capitalism if exploitation can still continue today. One option is to close our borders, send many non-residents back, and simply pay more for grapes and products that are not processed by their cheap labor. The only other defendable option is to provide fairness to this sub-lower-class, and that will definitely cost something extra. And the only apparent ways to cover those costs are higher taxes on somebody, increased national debt, or serious sharing of some of our super-affluence (as mentioned in the Nehemiah Proposals and included in Capitalism-21).

Race and national origin are major characteristics of the various waves of immigration, so we do need to acknowledge those roots. However, please note that ethnic origin and race are NOT the basis of America's prosperity and poverty. Instead, in today's America, the major class distinction is in terms wealth, as expressed in "socio-economic status." But socio-economic class is also highly related to education and intelligence.

Education and Intelligence

By definition, half of the American population is below average in intelligence. However, probably those in the middle two-thirds (67%) are so similar to each other that differences are not very noticeable even in terms of wealth and status because of other variables such as personal drive, will power, inheritance, and even health. At the top end, a very intelligent person has a better the chance for a higher-quality education plus its benefits for employment and wealth. This relates to talent, the fourth way to become wealthy. These people have advantages, but that is how life is [but it should not be exploitive or abusive].

At the extreme lower end, we find the severely mentally challenged people, and our society does offer services and assistance for them. In the next slightly higher group are many millions who fall between the cracks. They are the dim, the slow-witted, the ones who struggled mentally in school with low "C" grades even in the "slower" or "assisted" classrooms in the best school districts. They are with us and they have problems that are not adequately addressed.

But there is still another third (100 million people) of the American population who have various degrees of mental difficulties confronting complicated tax forms, health options, banking, job training, and retirement plans. Adjectives for them include "semi-skilled," "unskilled" (by ability, not by choice like some lazy smart ones), and "vulnerable." Some elements in our society will entice them with credit-card debt, sub-prime minimal down-payment mortgages, the empty rhetoric of negative political campaigns to elect serial-incumbents, and occasionally manipulative leadership seeking personal advantages. And the prospects can be disastrous for those people and, cumulatively, for the nation. However, theoretically pure capitalism allows, encourages, and thrives on the notion that those who can do things better should benefit at the expense of those who cannot.

And here I say "whoa, our system is out of balance." In our materialistic Capitalism-20 society, the cards are truly stacked against those who have less mental ability. All the educational assistance in the world cannot turn a slow-learner into a mental wizard. Besides, our country needs the variety of skills and attitudes that match with different job types. People are not created equal in all aspects, and our economic system needs to be fairer in such situations.

◇◇

All Americans have received some benefits from the "exploitation" of other people in America. Our prosperity has been built on the shoulders of all Americans before us, including the ancestors of those in need today.

◇◇

My main point is that all of us Americans have received some benefits from the "exploitation" of other people in America. And our personal prosperity does not alter or justify the fact that some people are less fortunate, even being in substandard circumstances. And those of us who enjoy the wondrous financial well-being of the middle-class and upper-class and super-class in America must recognize that this prosperity has been built on the shoulders of all Americans before us, including the ancestors of those in need today. We must get the lower end of our house in order. Otherwise we have failed some of our own people. We need to have our own house in order if we desire to be now and in the future a leading prosperous and great nation.

The "lower classes" come from low income, which leads to poor living conditions, inferior schools, and crime-ridden neighborhoods which, in turn, often lead to poor social skills which disqualify job-seekers from any but the lower-paying jobs. And, this cycle for "lower classes" continues with each generation. The wealthy people who are white, black, brown, red, yellow or whatever color or origin must pay attention to the needs of the less fortunate members of our society without regard to race or origin. Period. This is crucial if America is to remain a great nation for decades and centuries to come.

Concerning capitalism, free enterprise is a crucial component. Free enterprise is good, but free enterprise with compassion is better. Far better!!! Capitalism-21 will be good for America the nation and for all Americans, whether rich, poor or in between. So says

I. M. Nehemiah
Of immigrant origins

Lowest Acceptable Living in America and the World
[Paper No. 13 of the Nehemiah Papers]
I. M. Nehemiah © March 2008

The First Goal of I. M. Nehemiah was stated in Paper No. 1:

Goal 1. Attain at least a minimal acceptable living for all people in America and in the World. This Paper No. 13 is an initial attempt to identify some socio-economic goals to be accomplished in America and in the World. I examine the levels of living and then suggest some minimum levels that are quite low, just high enough to give people a decent chance for fairness. Feel free to disagree (or maybe agree?) with what I have written. Discussion is healthy.

Because people naturally desire to have more and more and more, all the way up to the very top rung, it might be useful to define what is and what is not included in the lowest acceptable living conditions in America, and also in the World. Example: Is an outhouse/latrine sufficient, or is a flush toilet required for a minimum bathroom, or is a Jacuzzi-style hot tub part of the standard for all people to attain? I have identified thirteen "Basics for Living" and ten "Levels of Living" to help determine what is "minimal."

<u>Thirteen (13) broad "Basics for Living"</u> are considered under three groupings:
Survival Basics:
  Water, Food, Clothing, Housing
Decency Basics:
  Safety/Freedom, Health, Sanitation, Education, Employment
Development Basics:
  Energy, Transportation, Communication, Finances

Ten (10) "Levels of Living" or "Socio-Economic Classes" in three groups.

> **In Affluence:**
>> Super-Upper Class, Upper Class, Middle Class, High-Lower Class
>
> **In the Boundary Between Affluence and Poverty:**
>> Low-Lower (USA = Min Acceptable), Sub-Lower for USA, World Minimum Acceptable
>
> **In Poverty:**
>> World-level Poverty, Ultra Poverty, Totally Destitute

All of these thirteen "Basics for Living" are cross tabulated with the ten "Levels of Living" to give 130 cells to show the "attainments" of how people live in affluent and impoverished societies. This table is presented as Figure 13-1 on the next two-page spread.

The "attainments" in the data cells cannot be strictly quantified in monetary terms. For example, in education (column H), actual dollar amounts spent per elementary school child have significant differences in cost and salaries between the major regions of America (and around the World). Instead, I have used qualitative terms that will eventually require more study and discussion than I can do in this essay.

There can be substantial overlap between vertically adjoining cells. Also there can be shifts upward or downward concerning what is appropriate for each "Level of Living." Certainly there is room for improvement of the table's information. I will not discuss every cell. Instead I provide a few summary statements.

How People Attain the Levels

The "attainments" of each level can be material (houses, shoes, *etc.*), immaterial (education, health, *etc.*), or communal attributes (communications, safety, sanitation, *etc.*). Sometimes these overlap, as in communities providing physical schools for personal education.

Also, the "attainments" can be derived from efforts by individuals, families, communities, state/national governments, and combinations of efforts. Interestingly, individualism is the strongest at both the very highest and very lowest levels. The personal drive to attain extreme wealth is matched by the personal drive to overcome bad water, build a shack, or learn to read without having a school. The need for survival is a great motivator.

Different from individualism, the efforts of societies and governments are aggregate and impact both the rich and the poor, but not equally. Typically, highways and telecommunications systems that are needed for the national well-being span generally large geographic areas, impact more people, and attract significant investments. Roads connect the important centers where the well-to-do are located but must cross through some distressed areas that are then uplifted by the new road. In America, our infrastructure base is so large that most citizens are served reasonably well. The combination of individual efforts and societal/governmental efforts elevate perhaps 80% of Americans are in the top four Levels of Living (Classes). What we consider to be standard middle class (nice home, safe neighborhood, private car(s), health care, good education, etc.) is enjoyed by only the top 20% of people in many developing countries.

In contrast in the developing countries, the relatively few corridors of services grow while other areas remain out of reach of the roads and other desired attributes. For example, large water projects with dams and hydroelectric generation benefit the national interests, but mainly serve the well to do. Electricity lines and water mains can literally go overhead and underneath people who have no access to those benefits. In general, electricity, water, hospitals, police, schools, *etc.* are more accessible and at relatively low subsidized per-unit costs for the affluent than they are for the needy. For example, taking a long hot bath with many gallons of treated water heated by electricity costs very little for a person living in an established neighborhood. But overall "costs" are disproportionately high in a minimum neighborhood where fewer gallons of the same water are manually carried for cooking and drinking and less-clean water is heated in a basin over a wood fire (because there is insufficient income for electricity even if sufficient electrical power was available). Essentially, the benefits from the government-assisted infrastructure projects are disproportionately delivered to the people who have the most, and the lesser fringe benefits fall to the disadvantaged people.

Figure 13-1: How People Live in Affluent Societies and in Impoverished Societies

	Survival Basics				Decency Basics	
There can be many transitions and overlaps between the vertically adjoining descriptions.						
Levels of Living (Classes)	Water A	Food B	Clothing C	Housing D	Safety / Freedom E	Health F
1 Super-Upper	Everything with water incl. yachts	Lavish dining	Designer fashions (no wild animal fur)	More than one home of great value	Law suits favoring lax-ity of rules	Physicians available on private calls
2 Upper	Jacuzzi and private pools	Imported specials	Imported fashions	Large homes and gardens	Security systems	Cosmetic surgery
Above this line, the words "lavish" and "extravagant" generally apply.						
3 Middle	Water parks & abundant water	Excessive choices	Fancy And with styles	Separate bedrooms + spare rooms	Very safe neighbor-hoods	Discretion-ary health choices
4 High-Lower	Plentiful water/ swimming pools	Good variety	Many choices	Modest own-ershipseveral rooms	Safe neigh-borhoods	Health insurance coverage
Above this line, the true needs are satisfied, but desires and "wants" for upward mobility are notorious. [Perhaps 80% of Affluent Societies, but less than 20% of the whole World.]						
5 Low-Lower USA = Min Acceptable	Hot and cold running	Sufficient in all ways	Abundant basics	Minimum spare space	Weak secruity	Public aid Medicaid
6 Sub-Lower for USA	Unreliable supply	Sufficient but some-times un-balanced	Abundant basics by charity	Slums & tenements	Dangerous neighbor-hoods	No health care; poor hygiene
7 World Minimum Acceptable	Clean and close to carry	Sufficient basic calories	Covered with locally correct	One or two rooms per family	Free, but with weak security	Minimum preventive medicine in society
Above this line are the boundaries of acceptable minimum standards. [In many developing societies, the "middle class" has the USA "Low-Lower" level of living.]						
8 World-level Poverty	Clean but far to carry	Minimal & unbalanced	Impoverish covering	Shack, often without land rights	Unsafe, trapped, endangered	Preventable diseases are common
9 Ultra Poverty	Contam-inated	Insufficient calories	No shoes, minimum clothes	Tent, squat-ter shacks	Victimized refugee	Chronic illness
10 Totally Destitute	None	Starvation	Wraps and rags	None	Slave	Severe diseases

Many refinements to this table are possible.						
Decency Basics			**Development Basics**			
Sanitation G	Education H	Employ-ment I	Energy J	Transpor-tation K	Commu-nication L	Finances M
Manicured and sterilized	Prestigious; personalized training by experts	Ownership or top management	Lavish use of energy	Luxury vehicles; 1st class travel	Multiples of all communications	Mega money and assets
Very clean	Private & high quality; advanced degrees	Business exec / owner & Profession	Little thought of energy	Fancy cars; much air travel	Top quality communications	Quite wealthy
[Perhaps 20% in Affluent Societies, but less than 5% of the whole World.]						
Clean environment	College expected; quality HS	Mixed white and blue collar	Consider electricity plentiful & basic	Good condition vehicles	Constant available communication	Very comfortable w/ discretionary income
Treated sewage	"Head-start" plus reasonable K-12	Blue-collar	Much electric; expensive	Used vehicles	Telephone & Internet	Comfortable w/ little extra money
In the three rows below, the needs are met in "minimal" ways that require careful definitions in the context of the different societies. [Perhaps 50% of the whole World.]						
Flush toilets & sewers	Reasonable K-12	USA minimum wage	Electricity in home	Public transp. or older cars	Telephone & television	Minimal funds; need to budget
Unreliable cleanliness	Substandard USA schools	Partial employ or unemploy.	Unreliable or lacking	Unable to move well	Marginal contacts	Always short for basics
Latrines; some waste removal	K-10 w/ low resources	Low-wage work	Clean cooking; No elect.	Some public transport	Minimal access phone & letters	Sufficient for local conditions, no extras
Below this line are the absolutely unacceptable conditions. [Perhaps zero % of Affluent Societies, but more than 30% of the whole world; that is over 2 billion people.]						
Minimal waste removal	Some elem. schooling	Partial employment	Solids + some LPG & liquids	Difficult transport, seldom very far	Limited outside contacts	At edge of monetary society
Polluted locality	Poor elem. schooling	Subsistence	Solid fuels	Walk, Maybe w/ animal	Talk, mainly local	Mainly barter
None	None	None	Scarce	Walk, few trails	Talking	No money, no assets

Home-life Basics

Housing, including Water, Sanitation and Energy: In America, housing should be structurally safe. Housing can be rented or owned and within the financial means of the family or individual. Except in very special circumstances, we expect functional hot and cold running water, electricity connection, kitchen with stove – refrigerator – sink, flush toilet, and heating appropriate to the geographic area. Although studio units are acceptable, most housing would have one or more bedrooms with usually no more than two persons in one bedroom.

◇◇

In the World's impoverished areas, clean drinking water, an efficient clean-burning cookstove and a latrine would be life-changing improvements.

◇◇

In the impoverished sectors of the World, to simply have clean drinking water is a major accomplishment. A clean-burning cooking stove and a latrine would be appreciated. The house might be of raw cement blocks and even have a thatched roof. A door and window that can be closed in bad weather would be nice.

Food: Nobody is to go hungry in America. But food stamps should be limited to more basic foods. Instruction about nutrition, especially for children, should be included in any food assistance efforts. Food assistance that is abused (such as for supporting drug addiction or alcoholism) should come with mandatory monitoring and rehabilitation.

The fact that malnourishment is still a problem in some parts of the World is an indictment of all people who live in the affluent societies, including the well-to-do people in the impoverished countries. Shame, Shame, Shame on us all.

Societal Basics

Education: As an absolute minimum, normal American children should have access to public K-12 schooling (Kindergarten through 12th grade) of sufficient quality to allow for normal progression to the next grade level, including possible entry into college studies or special training. The materials and instruction in one school should be at least adequate at an established minimum quality uniformly across the nation, as shown by the academic success of students who transfer between schools. Children with disabilities receive additional assistance. The buildings are to be safe and also up to minimum standards. Class sizes should be reasonably uniform nationwide. The above does not apply to private schools. There are no voucher systems to remove only a small number of students to private or select schools; education is not a lottery. This mandate applies to the core curriculum (including physical education and some fine arts) but does not extend to organized sports or excessive "refinement courses." Transportation to and from school is to be provided for all students beyond walking distance. There is no justification for dismal quality in American K-12 education.

To provide the above-described education to all children around the World would be a worthy but overly idealistic goal. Instead, I simply say that all children should obtain up to a 10th grade education in an organized educational setting with at least minimal resources such as textbooks and teachers and probably desks in appropriately enclosed buildings. In reality, such a minimal acceptable education is very far from being accomplished for literally hundreds of millions of children, especially girls and anyone with even mild learning difficulties. We have much work to do.

Health: American health systems need to be both accessible and affordable. Details for health coverage for essential health issues for all Americans are being included under various plans to be proposed and debated in 2009. The benefits do not need to cover non-essential treatment, to be defined by experts in the field. Major medical coverage is important, but organ transplants and other highly expensive treatments are not automatically covered. We are trying to keep people healthy, not prolong lives by every means possible. Medicines are to be available and affordable.

In the developing societies, health care is almost a tragic joke. Some major health problems in significant areas could be dramatically altered by financial resources of one or a few of the World's hundreds of billionaires.

◇◇◇

Please look again at Figure 13-1 and point to your level in each of the columns, creating a line across the table. Be thankful for where you are at and think about people living below your line.

◇◇◇

For example, provide artificial limbs to the tens of thousands of landmine victims. 100,000 prosthetic legs at $50 each (which is high) would cost only 5 million dollars. EACH of our major presidential candidates generated over ten times that amount every month or two just for the campaign costs. Shame on our current form of capitalism for allowing thousands of people to add five million dollars to their net worth each year while this and other solvable problems still exist. Maybe I did not say that correctly. How about this: Shame on anyone who has a net worth increase of five million dollars or more per year who does not have his or her own assistance program of at least one million dollars per year to bring some major benefits to landmine victims (or victims of some other serious problem).

Safety/Freedom: Safety in the American workplace is well under control. Safety issues in America's problem neighborhoods need massive intervention. Basically neighborhoods need non-fearful freedom of movement from 5 AM to 11 PM to allow people to do essential activities. During the other hours, at least cautious or escorted movement should be available. This will be a major undertaking far more difficult than attaining the education, housing, food, and health minimums. Elsewhere I write about crackdowns on crime, drugs, *etc.* that are needed to accompany the provision of safety.

When America and Europe and other affluent countries are compared to the rest of the World about safety and freedom, we are extremely fortunate. Criminality in many other (but not all) societies is extremely bad. Why? There are many factors, but three stand out to me.

A. Poverty. Being poor is not an excuse for being bad, but poverty certainly lowers the resistance to temptations of taking things from others, or doing acts such as drug trafficking.

B. Low ethical standards. When the leadership in some countries has a long tradition of abuse and low morals, the masses of people are likely to follow that course.

C. Poor education. Low education levels compound into low pay jobs and low or false self-esteem. Instruction of what is correct and incorrect behavior is difficult when education is absent or even prohibited to provide moral guidance.

Note: This is strange!!! I wrote the above three points about the impoverished countries and now I see them as being totally applicable to America also!! Woe is us.

There are several more topics to write about, but today I am tired. The issues about what is "acceptable poverty" are all so heavy. In America we are far from accomplishing what needs to be done. And there is so much that also must be done in the other areas of the World. Maybe some other day I will write more because

I. M. Nehemiah
Warrior against poverty in America and the World

Four Nehemiah Articles
of April 2016
[Papers No. 14-A through 14-D
of the Nehemiah Papers]
I. M. Nehemiah © 2016

These four articles that now are Paper No. 14 were originally released separately. Article 1 is dated 13 April 2016; the other three articles are dated 26 April 2016. All four articles were licensed under the _Creative Commons Attribution-NonCommercial-NoDerivatives 4.0 International License_. And placed at: _http://capitalism21.org/articles_

Factual information in the articles was obtained from Wikipedia articles on the topics in 2016.

Article 1: Paper 14-A **Variations in American Capitalism**

Article 2: Paper 14-B **Democracy at Risk**

Article 3: Paper 14-C **Unbalanced Powers in America**

Article 4: Paper 14-D **American National Service by All**

Variations in American Capitalism
[Paper No. 14-A of the Nehemiah Papers]
I. M. Nehemiah © April 2016

America's economy is based on Capitalism – a system that has evolved through four major variations and is currently positioned for another shift.

In 1776 Adam Smith published his famous book "The Wealth of Nations," explaining the then-new economic system of Capitalism as *an economic and political system in which a country's trade and industry are controlled by private owners for profit, rather than by the state.* [Wikipedia]. Smith also wrote about "Moral Sentiments" (1759) that would help keep in check the self-interests of greed, abuse of power, etc. [This is the basis of Capitalism-17.]

But morality without authority could not regulate the initial "Unbridled Capitalism" [of Capitalism-18. By the 1890s, virtually unrestricted *laissez-faire* ("leave alone") Capitalism-18 produced the robber barons, monopolies, trusts, Gilded Age, and vast differences between the few with extreme wealth, masses in poverty, and a rather small middle class.

Reactions against these greedy (but mainly legal) abuses initiated the century-long second variation with "Regulated Capitalism" [Capitalism-19] shifting toward governmental supervision, including trust-busting, progressive income taxes, bank regulation, Keynesian economics, social security, recognition of labor unions, and (with social as well as economic factors) women's rights and civil rights for equality.

Among the leaders advocating and accomplishing reforms to accomplish Regulated Capitalism [Cap-19] were the wealthy Republican politician

Teddy Roosevelt (President, 1901 to 1909) and his Democrat cousin Franklin D. Roosevelt (President, 1933 to 1945). The socio-economic controls were 1) the self-imposed products of democratically-elected governments, and 2) were clearly not in the realm of Socialism where *ownership is communal rather than by private individuals.*

The next major variation was the rise of "Conservative Capitalism" [Cap-20] and its hero, Ronald Reagan (President, 1981 to 1989). Conservatives essentially reversed many reforms set in place to control Capitalism: income tax rates slashed, regulations lifted on financial institutions, labor unions weakened, increased deficit spending that falsely boosted the economy, reduction of various public services, and increased hardships on people who were less-endowed financially, socially or mentally.

◇◇◇

Conservative Capitalism [Capitalism-20] is associated with substantial swings where record-high stock markets favor those with more resources and subsequent down-swings hurt especially the employee-class.

◇◇◇

Conservative Capitalism [Capitalism-20] is associated with substantial swings where record-high stock markets favor those with more resources. A new "Gilded Age" returned for a privileged few. Bill Clinton (President, 1993 to 2001) yielded to a conservative Congress. Lack of regulation caused down-swings like the Savings-and-Loan-Crisis and the Great Recession, after which the wealthy further increased their wealth and power. Obama was a "recovery" President (2009-2017) whose signature legislation for affordable health care ("Obamacare") left big business in charge of prescription drugs, insurance, and most medical services, with the focus on profits still trumping concerns for human wellbeing.

So we arrive at the 2016 Election Year with a full array of advocates for different variations of Capitalism. Columnist Charles Krauthammer (March 31, 2016) *https://www.washingtonpost.com/opinions/the-four-foreign-policies/2016/03/31/bf28a7e6-f764-11e5-a3ce-f06b5ba21f33_story.html* characterized Ted Cruz as being most similar to Ronald Reagan, and therefore a "Conservative Capitalist" who is against government regulation of business. If elected President, Cruz would accentuate Reaganomics with free-wielding business practices, less environmental protection, and social values of the Tea Party evangelical minority, especially if Republicans control Congress and if the Supreme Court lacks balance.

The same article quite correctly labels Donald Trump a "mercantilist," akin to King Philip II who expanded the Spanish Empire (1556 to 1598). Mercantilism is what existed after Feudalism and before Unrestricted Capitalism. Mercantilism is *the economic theory that trade generates wealth and is stimulated by the accumulation of profitable balances, which a government should encourage by means of protectionism* [Wikipedia] or geo-political influence.

If elected President, Trump's vision to "Make America Great Again" would change the face of American economic policy to that of an international bully, a tough guy who gets his own way or will not play. Would Congress or the courts go along, or try to prevent his damage? [Note: This was written in April 2016.]

Hillary Clinton is characterized by Krauthammer as a political continuation of Presidents Bill Clinton and Obama for international and social issues. In terms of the economics of Capitalism, that places her as weakly resisting Reagan's Conservative Capitalism. If elected President, Hillary would continue as part of the establishment that joins together the wealthy of both political parties to perpetuate the status quo. Disastrous Congress-versus-President struggles would probably continue.

On economic issues, Bernie Sanders is simultaneously a refreshing inspiration and a nightmare. He created the nightmare by self-declaring to be a Socialist, which he certainly is not. [See *https://en.wikipedia.org/wiki/Political_positions_of_Bernie_Sanders*] And because true Socialism is appalling to Americans over 50 years old, Bernie is unwittingly throwing away millions of votes. But he does appeal to those who are 40 or younger; after all, they were less than 15 years old or unborn when the Soviet Union broke apart in 1991. They do not know any better, and Sanders is not doing a good job of educating them about what is true Socialism, a la Karl Marx.

Krauthammer likened Sanders to George McGovern, the very liberal Democrat defeated by Nixon in the 1972 presidential election. But Sanders can also be likened to Republican Teddy Roosevelt, whose efforts to break up the ultra-powerful financial elite and to protect the environment are both cornerstones of the Sanders political platform.

As was Teddy 115 years ago, Bernie could be a forerunner of a major shift in Capitalism, back toward "Regulated Capitalism" but with Twenty-First Century attributes. Modern times require modern solutions, and Sanders is proposing many changes that could bring Capitalism in America back on track with some of Adam Smith's moral integrity.

If elected President, Sanders must work with Congress to bring about economic justice within 21st Century Capitalism [Capitalism-21].

Democracy at Risk
[Paper No. 14-B of the Nehemiah Papers]
I. M. Nehemiah © April 2016

Democracy is America's chosen form of governance, not monarchy, dictator-ship or anarchy. And Democracy is based on the recurring process of voting. Therefore, ALL laws and many aspects of American society can be changed by simply voting for changes.

We can even vote for changes about voting. Originally, only adult male, property-owning, free persons could vote, but eventually the electorate expanded to include non-property owners (by 1856), all free males (1860s), women (1920), and individuals aged 18 to 21 (1971). Poll taxes were elim-inated in 1964.

But there still remain some aspects of voter disenfranchisement. For instance, ten states permanently ban felons from voting, even after serving their sentences. And gerrymandering is still legal to give geographical ad-vantage or disadvantage to some candidates or constituents.

Also, because the only votes counted are from eligible voters who are actually present (or who have submitted absentee ballots), a long-standing "trick" to win elections is to prevent opposing people from voting. This can be done by using physical intimidation, legalistic complications, corruption, or inconvenience (location and number of polling places, as in the 2016 Arizona primary elections). Whenever democracy is denied to persons, Democracy of the nation is at risk.

With a few exceptions for very small groups (such as clubs and busi-ness partners), democratic governance is usually by elected representatives (ranging from members of a board of directors to members of Congress) and elected executives (governors and Presidents). The representatives are empowered to vote (and executives can take direct action) on behalf of their constituents.

Essentially, the people can have their say, and then the elected ones can have their way. Since elected representatives can pass laws that increasingly favor certain positions, those who influence elected officials with money, lobbying and endorsements can alter the direction of the nation. The money of our Capitalist Economic System is overpowering our Democratic Governance System.

Note that this discussion is not about the election **process**; it is about efforts devised to ensure [that] elected **politicians** favor a specific point of view when laws and rules are being decided.

In 2010 the traditional and legal restrictions limiting anonymous political donations by corporations were removed by the U.S. Supreme Court split-decision (5 to 4) on a campaign finance case by "Citizens United" (a non-profit **organization** that promotes **corporate** interests). Now Super PACs (Political Action Committees) roam freely to establish their influence over elected persons by donations and campaign announcements, presented as freedom of speech under First Amendment protection.

For example, Big Oil (large oil companies) can support candidates from either political party who would favor fossil fuel usage, and vigorously oppose those who are anti-Big Oil or favor environmental protection and renewable energy. Impersonal, non-living, profit-motivated corporate entities use business muscle to alter the opinions of voters, placing Democracy at risk.

The American tradition of having only two major political parties is becoming detrimental because the elected legislators are increasingly controlled by party leadership that influences the longevity and success of their political careers. Voting along "party lines" is infamous when key issues are being discussed, and anyone who steps out of line faces drastic consequences from their party elders/leaders. Term limits would end the abuses of "serial incumbents."

Having "control" (a simple majority) in the House of Representatives and/or the Senate has become a blunt weapon for holding hostage the legislative interests and proposals of a President (or state governor) who is of the opposing party. National examples abound. At state level, Illinois has gone ten months without a budget (as of April 2016), with no sign of compromise.

◇◇◇

America needs a modest number of truly independent elected legislators who can prevent partisan Republican and Democrat majorities and can represent the wishes of America's moral center.

◇◇◇

America does not need a third political party. What it needs is a modest number of truly independent elected legislators. Ten percent (10%) would be sufficient. Ten U.S. Senators and forty-three Representatives could take control of Congress by voting with constructive reasoning. This would strengthen Democracy in America. [Five percent or even two percent could be sufficient, if truly independent of either major political party and in the moral center.]

Nothing is perfect. Politics tend to be dirty with many "under the table" (but not illegal) dealings. Rules are made. Rules can be changed. Two examples from the current 2016 Presidential Primary Elections in America are:

1. Republicans: Donald Trump missed the boat on the selection of the delegates to the Republican Convention. Winning in a state's primary does not mean that the delegates selected to attend the convention will be loyal to Trump after the first ballot. Regardless of Trump's complaints, the rules were there all along. It is as if a businessman did not fully read a business contract before he signed it. It is not unfair.

2. Democrats: Concerning Black voters and southern Democrats, Hillary Clinton has a massive popularity advantage over Bernie Sanders. This translated into her winning of 701 vs. Sanders' 331 pledged delegates in the eleven southern-state primary elections, an advantage of 370 delegates to help her win the party's nomination.

However, based on decades of solid southern voting for Republicans, neither Clinton nor Sanders is likely to win more than two or three of those eleven southern states in the November general elections. Without those pledged southern-states delegates, Sanders would be approximately 130 pledged delegates ahead of Clinton at this time (post New York primary). The convention rules will not be changed, but perhaps the Super Delegates will see and act upon this reality of Sanders' superior numbers in northern and western states.

The good news is that American democracy allows for voting on changes to improve the system. While Democracy is always better than the alternatives, it is placed at risk whenever the population fails to defend and improve its implementation, including controls on the influence of money.

Unbalanced Powers in America
[Paper No. 14-C of the Nehemiah Papers]
I. M. Nehemiah © April 2016

There are "Five Realms of Power" in America (or in any country, organization, club or household). We have already introduced two powers (Economics and Governance) and have shown how Democracy and Capitalism are out of balance in America, with money influencing voting.

The powers are ideally separate but intertwined as societal forces. All five powers are always present, but not with equal strength. The powers and their predominant manifestations in America are:

1. **Governance** (Decision making): Democracy (not Dictatorship, etc.)
2. **Economics** (Financial structure): Capitalism (not Socialism, etc.)
3. **Religion** (Faith): Christianity (with several types, but none are official)
4. **Justice** (Legal enforcement): Written laws (not Anarchy, Scriptural, etc.)
5. **Love** (Caring systems): Service to others (not Self-service, Hate, Jealousy, etc.)

Note: **Physical power** is NOT named because the use of force could be commanded by any of the five realms, depending on circumstances. For example, five types of military forces could be units that are national, mercenary (hired), Jihadist or Crusader, UN peace-keeper, or disaster-rescue.

Religion: The power of religion is through its influence upon the believers of whatever "faith" they profess. "Believers" or "the faithful" answer to a "higher power" (generally called "God"). Their influence can increase by converting others to believe the same way, or through prayers.

Faith's influences upon the other four realms of power are through voting, financial expenditures/donations, seeking laws that reflect scriptural teachings, or by providing service to others. All such influence is legal and appropriate in America, where the power of religion has seen both high and low periods for influencing governance and economics.

However, America's separation of Church and State requires that Faith uses its power **indirectly** through influence on the other four realms to be compliant with religious values. Those values typically emphasize patriotism/duty-to-vote, hard work with no stealing/cheating, obedience to just laws, and ethical values that show love and caring. Difficulties can arise when specific "faiths" (brands of religion) have different interpretations of values (e.g., Pro-Life).

Justice: America is a nation governed by laws. Sometimes issues of "fairness" and "allowed behavior" require enforcement or recourse for review and correction, as specified by our legal system.

Police are employed to uphold the laws (and not overstep their authority). Motorists drive vehicles reasonably within the speed limits or face the consequences. Laws about deportation of illegal immigrants and about drug trafficking are subject to political debates and budget-controlled enforcement.

However, Justice (fairness) can be distorted when laws favor wealth accumulation by those who are already extremely rich and powerful. Justice is not served when governance (such as the elected U.S. Senate) can simply decline to do its appointed functions (such as reviewing nominations for a Supreme Court Justice vacancy).

American laws specify that a person can "have his day in court" for possible rectification of injustices. However, our laws do not guarantee a favorable solution. People with deeper pockets can more easily prevail in courts of law, showing the unbalance between economic power (money) and the power of Justice for fairness.

Love: The power of love is everywhere. There are countless songs about it. Wonderful examples of caring occur and sometimes are heralded in the media.

Love and caring interact with and influence the other four realms of power in several ways. Expressed as "caring for justice", love influences how and what American laws are written. The sense of fairness eventually gathered sufficient votes (governance) with constitutional amendments and laws (legal actions) to overcome the dark times of [slavery and] open segregation.

But financial inequalities within current American Conservative Capitalist [Capitalism-20] activities (economics) reveal some need for more caring (love) and more justice by laws for everyone. Issues include equal pay for women, changes in the graduated income tax rates, and aspects of health care and education.

The unbalances between the Five Realms of Power in America are primarily evident in the overpowering influence of money, the tool of relatively unrestrained economic Capitalism-20.

The unbalances between the Five Realms of Power in America are primarily evident in the overpowering influence of money, the tool of relatively unrestrained economic Capitalism-20. To accomplish more balance against the power of excessive money, American voters (Governance) can choose to have laws (Justice) to implement more caring (Love) within the society.

The above comments can be documented. What we need are serious actions that can help remedy the unbalances. Please consider the context and merits of the following.

It is proposed that America utilize "compulsory national service" as a tool to assist society and all individuals. Service to the nation can be service to others (Caring) with many beneficial results.

America prides itself on service (Love/Care/Volunteer/Donate) through patriotism (governance), giving to charities (economics), fairness of laws (justice), and its embrace of the fundamentals of Christian faith. But there is one overshadowing problem: service contributions are voluntary, inequitably preformed, and poorly rewarded.

Military service is voluntary, involves very few people, and the ranks are typically filled by lower- and middle-class citizens. Also, social service jobs and even teaching are relatively poorly paid professions that are strongly impacted by budget cuts.

Financially, vast numbers of Americans donate to churches and charities, but amounts are generally sporadic, small, and very influenced by marketing. For example, Veterans Organizations and Police Officer Associations use telemarketing to pay for what taxpayers are unwilling to provide.

Many people abuse the legal system if (or as long as) they can get away with it. That is why those in banking and hedge fund trading in America do not want government regulation or monitoring. And others want to reduce or eliminate government services (less government intervention) ranging from food inspection and social safety to audits of tax evaders and environmental protection. History repeatedly shows that fairness and quality control cannot be left to self-monitoring.

Even service-minded entities (churches, charities, etc.) often fail at self-monitoring by paying high executive salaries, diverting services and funds to preferred beneficiaries, and doing more "preaching of their faith" (using tax-deductible donations) than actually providing services to the needy.

ALL of the above mentioned deficiencies could be largely resolved with a program of compulsory national service. (See next article.)

American National Service by All
[Paper No. 14-D of the Nehemiah Papers]
I. M. Nehemiah © April 2016

Dear Readers: This article utilizes content from three previous articles in a published series at capitalism21.org, so some statements are condensed to keep this article brief. All aspects of this proposal are open for discussion.

The Five Realms of Power are Governance, Economics, Religion, Justice and Love. Their respective "currencies" for actions are votes, money, beliefs, laws, and service.

The realms of power are out of balance in America, with money exercising enormous influence over the other realms. The excessively disproportionate influence of money impacts our elections, compromises our elected representatives, warps our national budgets, alters the activities of religious groups, distorts our laws, and changes our views of service.

Greed, selfishness, and pride have led to the imbalance of power. One possible antidote is service, more service, and much more service.

The proposal is that *service* for the national wellbeing must be compulsory for everyone, according to laws to be enacted, with constitutional amendments if necessary.

There will be many variations of this service, according to the abilities of the citizens and the needs of our society. Implementation requires diligent work and attention to thousands of details. The presentation here focuses on the intended outcomes.

1. Service is by Americans of ***all*** ages and both genders, excluding only the very young, the very elderly, and the truly infirm.
   A. School children in grades K – 12 would have activities to learn about service as well as to do service.
   B. Young adults (ages 17 – 26) would have two years of service with a very wide range of options, as discussed below.
   C. Adults (ages 27 – 54) would have special opportunities, many related to assisting other families and local communities.
   D. Seniors (ages 55 – 80) would have "Honor Service" events, etc. appropriate for their circumstances.
2. Much (perhaps 25%) of the service will be for the implementation and guidance and quality control of the service of others. This results in high quality administration at rock bottom costs.
3. Much (perhaps 25%) of the service will be in the acquisition (learning) of valuable skills, essentially a form of volunteer interns who are becoming more employable while doing their service to the nation.
4. Service to the nation can have many forms, including military (combat), military (construction), Peace Corps, AmeriCorps, modernized Civilian Conservation Corps (CCC of the 1930s), and special programs that could be approved according to stringent requirements.
5. Citizens in selected employment fields of service with low pay (examples: social work, education, security, health care) can receive service credit by completing 6 or 8 years in those careers.

Specifics for the Young Adult Service Corps:

Every male and female American citizen (and possibly all resident aliens) between the ages of 18 and 26 years, will perform a total of 24 months (or perhaps more) of training and/or work in the authorized and supervised "American National Service Corps" programs. Allowances will be given for flexible time schedules to satisfy this requirement. These will be "sworn in" positions.

Basic military training is required for at least 6 months. Non-combatant options (such as medics) will be available for conscientious objectors and for those with physical challenges. Numerous American military bases that are currently closed will be re-activated. Training will include instruction on citizenship, American freedoms and values, disaster response, and homeland security.

All branches of the US Military Services will be expanded and will include Task Forces for Development (TFDs) such as for road building and environmental protection. Deployment of units will be as deemed appropriate for the wellbeing of the United States and its international relationships (with expected co-lateral advantages for willing, participating foreign nations).

Options in the greatly expanded Peace Corps, AmeriCorps and new initiatives will be available for some, on a competitive basis, who have completed university degrees or have high-demand skills prior to their service time.

To the extent possible, these service months will include at least 30 days overseas in less-affluent foreign environments.

Implementation issues:

A one-year age cohort in America has approximately 4 million persons. This means that approximately 8 million "full-time positions" [including important training] will be created and be continually filled as young adults pass through their two years of national service. This is job creation at the national level with very low costs and high benefits to the nation and the individuals.

◇◇

Approximately 8 million "full-time positions" that include important training will be created and be continually filled as young adults pass through their two years of national service.

◇◇

Exposure to military discipline will help build core values of work ethics and patriotism. America will also be better prepared for difficult times, whether from conflicts, natural disasters, or challenged neighborhoods in need of assistance.

For many who might otherwise face unemployment after high school graduation, the service years also provide opportunities for training (and "internships") in skills and trades that will lead to employment afterwards.

For many who complete college academic degrees, their service years will provide opportunities to use their skills, many in entry-level jobs (including business skills and production work) that are supportive of other service projects.

Because of the separation of church and state in America, two years of service as proselytizing missionaries would not be counted, but humanitarian service work with a church group could be counted, subject to rules and monitoring.

The net result is a stronger America. Further articles will provide more details.

About the Author

I. M. Nehemiah is the allonym of one or more adult Americans who collectively write about America, as did three patriots in 1788 who wrote the Federalist Papers under the allonym of Publius. Ancient Nehemiah was the rebuilder of Jerrusalem around 440 BC. Modern I. M. Nehemiah works to rebuild America in the 21st Century. Dr. Paul S. Anderson is the compiler of this book and designated contact editor for the collective I. M. Nehemiah efforts. He can be reached at: editor@capitalism21.org

www.ingramcontent.com/pod-product-compliance
Lightning Source LLC
Chambersburg PA
CBHW032020170526
45157CB00002B/788